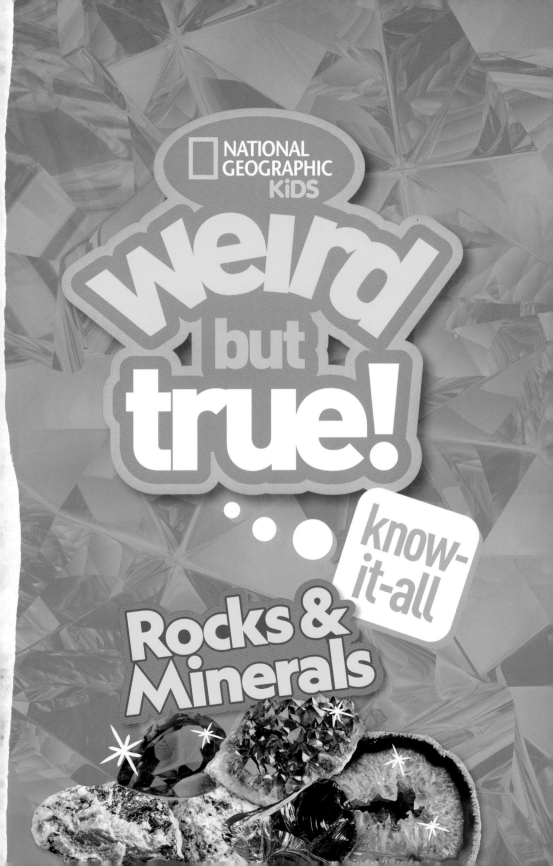

NATIONAL GEOGRAPHIC KiDS

weird but true!

know-it-all

Rocks & Minerals

NATIONAL GEOGRAPHIC KiDS

weird but true!

know-it-all

Rocks & Minerals

MICHAEL BURGAN

CONTENTS

ROCKING YOUR WORLD!

What does a tiny grain of sand have in common with a giant boulder? What do they both have in common with a pebble on a playground? Because you grabbed *this* book—and not one on, say, dinosaurs—you can probably guess: They're all rocks! Almost our entire planet is made up of rocks: Once you take away the air, water, and living things from the surface of our planet, what you're left with is pretty much a whole lot of rock. They come in many sizes and colors and are formed in different ways. You can spot them everywhere. Whether you're catching some rays on a beach, exploring a canyon, or just strolling down a city street, you're bound to come upon—or sometimes trip over!—rocks or something made from them.

And then there are the rocks we *can't* see, like the red-hot rock deep below Earth's surface and the rocky mountain ranges deep within the oceans' depths.

And, just in case you're wondering, there are plenty of rocks in outer space, too. Some are pieces of planets or smaller space objects called asteroids. The rocks break off from the planets or asteroids and hit Earth's atmosphere at speeds of up to 160,000 miles an hour (257,495 km/h)! The space rocks that make the journey all the way to Earth's surface are called meteorites. While they land all over the planet, many meteorites are found on Antarctica. The icy continent is very dry, so the meteorites aren't damaged by water in the air, as they are in most other regions. Plus, since Antarctica is covered in ice, the dark meteorites are easy to spot against the white surface.

Luckily for you, you don't have to go to Antarctica to see meteorites, or take a submarine ride to explore underwater mountains. Keep reading, as we leave no stone unturned to help you learn all about rocks ... wherever they're found!

Whoaaa

PAY DIRT!

By one estimate, Earth's deserts and beaches contain more than seven quintillion grains of sand—that's a seven followed by 18 zeros!

ROCK STARS
WHAT IS A GEOLOGIST?

Anyone can admire the rocks all around us, but it takes a specially trained person to dig up the dirt on the importance of rocks. A scientist who studies rocks and the minerals in them is called a geologist. Geologists also investigate how volcanoes erupt, where earthquakes are likely to shake things up, and where valuable natural resources are located. Throughout this book, you'll meet some of the "rock stars" who have helped uncover Earth's structure and history.

Let's rock and roll

Rocks make up every continent, mountain, and island on the planet. But what *is* rock?

In simple terms, a rock is a naturally occurring solid object usually made from minerals. Rocks are classified as one of three main types—igneous, sedimentary, and metamorphic—depending on how they're formed. A rock can also transform from one type to another; over millions of years, the processes of the rock cycle break it down or melt it, change it, and reform it into new rock.

MINERALS MATTER!

Within the three different categories of rocks, what makes one rock different from another are the ways the different minerals combine together. Rocks are usually made up of one or more minerals (see page 100 to learn more about minerals).

Minerals are made up of tiny particles called atoms, and these atoms are arranged in a particular pattern. This pattern creates what are called crystals. The crystals determine what a mineral looks like, and they can shape how a rock looks, too. These crystals can affect whether a rock is rough or smooth and how hard it is. Minerals also come in different colors, and that can affect a particular rock's appearance, too. A mineral called hematite can make a rock red or brown. It's this mineral that gives sandstone its brown tint. The mineral quartz gives rocks a range of colors, though they usually tend to be light shades of gray. Dacite—usually bluish gray or pale gray—is one rock that is often loaded with quartz.

• ROCK GLOSSARY •

Rocks and minerals may look simple, but there's a mountain of science that helps explain how they form and what they can do. To make sure you're on solid ground as you navigate the terrain, take a minute to familiarize yourself with these important terms:

ATOMS: Microscopic particles that are the basic unit of an element.

BACTERIA: Single-celled microorganisms thought to be the first forms of life on Earth.

CONDUCTOR: A material that transmits a form of energy, such as heat or electricity; some substances are better conductors than others.

CRYSTAL: The arrangement of tiny particles called atoms and molecules found in minerals; each mineral has its own crystal structure.

DORMANT: Referring to a volcano that has not erupted in a long time but might again someday.

ELEMENT: One of more than 100 substances on Earth that has a unique set of chemical and physical properties and that make up everything on the planet.

EROSION: The natural process through which wind, water, and ice wears away and removes rock and soil.

EXTINCT: In geology, refers to a volcano that no longer erupts.

FOSSIL: The remains of ancient life-forms, or traces or impressions of an organism, which are found in rocks.

FRACTURE: The way that minerals and rocks break apart or have a break within.

LANDFORM: A natural feature of Earth's surface, such as a mountain.

LUSTER: The way light reflects off a rock or mineral, which indicates how dull or brilliant it is.

MOLTEN: Turned into liquid by high heat.

MONOLITH: A single giant stone or rock.

NUCLEAR: Referring to the center, or nucleus, of an atom.

PROPERTIES: The particular traits of a specific rock or mineral.

QUARRY: A place from which large amounts of certain rocks are, or have been, removed, often for use in buildings; or the act of removing the rocks.

RADIATION: A form of energy released by some elements as they naturally change that can be harmful in large doses; materials with high levels of radiation are called radioactive.

SEDIMENT: Broken pieces of rock that can move from one place to another and often settle to the bottom of bodies of water.

TECTONIC: Relating to the structure of Earth's crust and mantle and the activity that takes place within them.

VITREOUS: A luster with a glassy look.

VOLCANOLOGIST: A geologist who specializes in the study of volcanoes.

THE ROCK CYCLE
• GOING 'ROUND AND 'ROUND •

A bicycle made of stone? Not quite. The rock cycle is the name for the process that describes how rocks form and change into different types of rocks over time. Rocks can form at any point in the cycle.

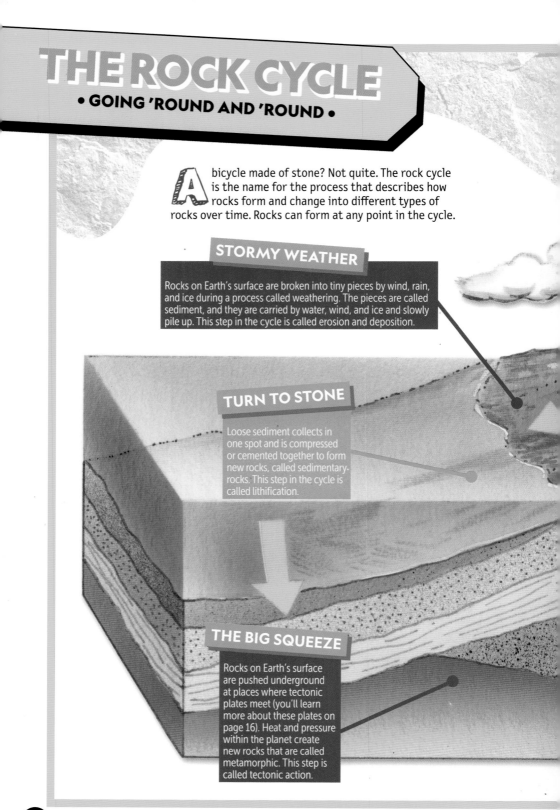

STORMY WEATHER

Rocks on Earth's surface are broken into tiny pieces by wind, rain, and ice during a process called weathering. The pieces are called sediment, and they are carried by water, wind, and ice and slowly pile up. This step in the cycle is called erosion and deposition.

TURN TO STONE

Loose sediment collects in one spot and is compressed or cemented together to form new rocks, called sedimentary rocks. This step in the cycle is called lithification.

THE BIG SQUEEZE

Rocks on Earth's surface are pushed underground at places where tectonic plates meet (you'll learn more about these plates on page 16). Heat and pressure within the planet create new rocks that are called metamorphic. This step is called tectonic action.

UNDERGROUND ACTION

Deep below Earth's surface, extreme heat turns minerals into a liquid called magma. Some cools slowly below Earth's surface, forming what are called intrusive, or plutonic, igneous rocks. Other magma reaches the surface and becomes the lava produced by a volcanic eruption. The lava cools quickly, forming extrusive, or volcanic, igneous rocks.

EARTH'S LAYERS
• WHAT LIES BENEATH •

If you jump up and down on the ground, everything seems solid beneath your feet. But if you could drill down toward the center of the planet, things would feel pretty soft—and very hot! Earth is made up of four main layers, and what's beneath the surface fuels volcanic eruptions and the rock cycle.

PAY DIRT!

Some areas between the inner and outer cores have temperatures of around 10,800°F (6000°C)—as hot as the surface of the sun!

CRUST

Bread isn't the only thing with a crust! The part of Earth right below you—a thin layer of rock that lies underneath both the continents and the oceans—is called the crust. It is made up of different elements, including oxygen, iron, and silicon.

MANTLE

Beneath the crust is the mantle. This layer contains rocks, but they're not totally solid and can move around. Some people have compared the consistency of the mantle to hot tar or gooey caramel.

A CORE GEOLOGIST

OUTER CORE

Deeper in the planet is Earth's core. The first part of it, the outer core, is made up mostly of liquid nickel and iron.

When an earthquake shakes Earth's surface, waves of energy ripple through the planet. Inge Lehmann was a Danish geologist who studied these seismic waves. When she was conducting research during the 1920s, most geologists thought Earth had a single liquid core. But after an earthquake hit New Zealand in 1929, Lehmann shook up the world of geology with a great discovery. She studied the movement of waves recorded at different scientific stations around the world and found that one type of seismic wave had reached Earth's surface at spots where scientists previously believed they couldn't. This created what was called a shadow zone. Lehmann believed that the waves had traveled into the core and were deflected by a solid inner core, creating a shadow zone where no waves hit. Later research proved she was right, that Earth's center has two parts—a solid inner core and a liquid outer core. The boundary that separates the two parts of the core was named for her: the Lehmann Discontinuity.

INNER CORE

At the very center of Earth is the inner core. This solid, round mass is made mostly of iron. The extreme temperatures in this metal ball would normally liquefy iron, but the pressure from the rest of the planet around it keeps it from melting.

BY THE NUMBERS
HOW THICK IS THAT?

CRUST	3–47 miles (5–76 km)
MANTLE	1,802 miles (2,900 km)
OUTER CORE	1,379 miles (2,220 km)
INNER CORE	758 miles (1,220 km)

ROCKS & WEATHER
• ROCKY RAINS AND WINDS •

I have ultimate power

Did you ever think that rocks could determine whether you need to put on a raincoat or a warm wool hat before you step outside? It's true—rocky landforms, such as mountains, can interact with winds to influence weather patterns. And mountains can make one region dry as a bone while another region nearby gets a good soaking.

COLD ON TOP

If you've ever climbed a mountain, you might have noticed that the temperature gets lower as you go higher. Air is cooler at the top of a mountain because it is less dense (thick) up there, so there are fewer air molecules to trap the heat. Also, infrared energy radiated by Earth's surface is the source of heat in the air. The higher you climb, the farther you get from the source of the heat.

It can also be windier on a mountaintop than on the ground below it. Close to the ground, a natural force called friction slows the moving air near the surface as it rubs against things like trees and buildings. But up on a mountain, there are fewer things for the air to rub against. That means the wind can really whip, which makes it feel chillier on top.

THE WET SIDE

A tall mountain range can also affect the weather for many miles on either side of its peaks. Let's take a virtual trip to the Cascade Range to see how this works. These mountains in the northwest United States sit to the east of the Pacific Ocean. Weather systems that form over the ocean can carry lots of water in them. Most of that moisture falls on the western side and on top of the mountains, as these weather systems move inland. After the air mass passes over the range, the air begins to warm. This warming reduces the humidity of the air so that there is less moisture to create rain and snow.

This helps explain why the western parts of Washington State get plenty of rain and snow, while some regions east of the mountains are deserts.

MOUNT BAKER IN WESTERN WASHINGTON RECEIVED A **RECORD 95 FEET** (29 M) **OF** SNOW DURING **JUST ONE YEAR.**

WHERE IN THE WORLD?
AS WET AS IT GETS

If you visit Mount Waialeale (pronounced why-AH-lay-AH-lay), be prepared to get drenched! At just over 5,140 feet (1,567 m) high, this mountain on the Hawaiian island of Kauai is the rainiest spot in the United States and the second wettest spot on the entire planet. In an average year, about 450 inches (1,143 cm) of rain fall on the mountain. You'd need a bucket taller than a telephone pole to collect that much water!

TECTONIC PLATES
• A PLATEFUL OF GEOLOGY •

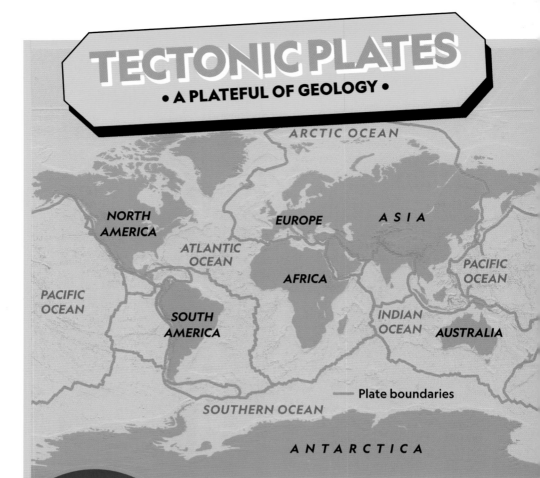

ARCTIC OCEAN

NORTH AMERICA

EUROPE

ASIA

ATLANTIC OCEAN

PACIFIC OCEAN

AFRICA

PACIFIC OCEAN

SOUTH AMERICA

INDIAN OCEAN

AUSTRALIA

— Plate boundaries

SOUTHERN OCEAN

ANTARCTICA

Some plates are just too big to eat from. Earth's crust is made up of large areas of rock called tectonic plates, which form the crust of continents and oceans. These plates rest on a soft part of the mantle that moves as it heats and cools, which moves the plates, too.

PUSH, PULL, AND SCRAPE

In the above map, you can see the tectonic plates. The place where two plates meet is called a boundary. Earth has about two dozen plates: seven large ones, six or seven medium-size ones, and several smaller ones.

The plates move around in different ways. Some plates push together at their boundaries, while others pull apart. Still others slide past each other. All this movement happens very slowly—a plate might move just two or three inches (5 to 8 cm) each year. But even though you can't feel that slow-motion movement under your feet as it's happening, you can observe the effects it has on Earth's surface.

PAY DIRT!

Because of Earth's constantly moving tectonic plates, Asia's Himalaya—home of Mount Everest—"grow" more than 0.4 inch (1 cm) a year!

Where two tectonic plates converge, or collide, with each other, mountains form. If one plate containing older ocean crust is pushed up against a plate with younger, lighter crust, then the plate with the older crust is usually forced back down into the mantle, forming a trench. Along the boundaries of the colliding plates, volcanoes form. Two separating, or diverging, plates often allow hot water, as geysers, to shoot out of the ground. Volcanoes form at divergent boundaries, too. Earthquakes occur at all types of plate boundaries, but especially at convergent ones.

WHEN PLATES COLLIDE

Most of North America sits on its own plate, which includes the continent's land and a big chunk of the Atlantic Ocean. The sliding of this plate against the nearby Pacific plate, which is under the Pacific Ocean, causes some of the earthquakes that strike California. Also off the Pacific Coast of North America is the Juan de Fuca plate. It's a small plate (more like a saucer!), and it sometimes slides beneath the larger North American plate next to it, which can also trigger earthquakes. Scientists say that the sliding of the Juan de Fuca plate under its bigger neighbor could someday spark some of the most powerful earthquakes ever to hit the continent.

The activity of tectonic plates in regions bordering the Pacific Ocean has produced some of the world's most violent earthquakes and destructive volcanic eruptions. This area has been called the Ring of Fire, though it's shaped more like a giant horseshoe. The Ring of Fire roughly follows the Pacific coasts of North and South America and East Asia and passes east of Australia. The ring is home to more than 450 volcanoes, and almost all the planet's major earthquakes take place there.

ROCK STAR
HE GOT THE DRIFT

Alfred Wegener didn't know about plate tectonics, but he had some pretty radical (for the time) ideas about moving continents. Wegener was a German scientist and explorer during the early 20th century. Looking at a world map, he observed that Earth's seven continents look as though they could fit together, like pieces of a jigsaw puzzle. He also noted that the fossils of some plants and animals found on one continent were very similar to ones on another continent, even though the continents were separated by vast oceans. Wegener suggested something considered shocking at the time: that the continents had at one time been a single giant "supercontinent" but had then drifted apart. He called this supercontinent Pangaea—ancient Greek for "all Earth." For decades, other scientists rejected this notion. But thanks to the work of Marie Tharp (see page 20) and others, scientists eventually learned that Earth is constantly creating new crust and that tectonic plates are always in motion. That knowledge showed that Wegener was right: Continents are in motion. Over the past billion years, Earth has had several supercontinents, with the movement of plates breaking them apart and then bringing them back together.

North Pole

Siberia

Ural Mts.

North China

Europe

PALEO-
TETHYS
OCEAN

North America

PANGAEA

Turkey

South China

South America

Iran

PANTHALASSIC
OCEAN

Africa

GONDWANA

TETHYS OCEAN

India

Australia

Antarctica

MARSQUAKES

• OUTTA SIGHT WITH INSIGHT •

PAY DIRT!

As of January 2021, InSight had recorded almost 500 marsquakes.

When you look to the stars, it's often easy to see Mars. On many nights, you can spot its red glow in the sky with the naked eye. Mars is called the red planet for that reason, and you actually have something in common with it. Iron, an element that helps make your blood red, is also found on that planet's surface. But what goes on underneath the surface of Mars? And what could that tell us about Earth's geology? That's what scientists are trying to figure out with the Mars InSight space mission.

ROCK STAR
ROCKIN' THE RED PLANET

At times, space objects called asteroids smash into Mars, breaking off pieces of the planet and sending them hurtling through space. Though it's rare, some of them reach Earth. And when they do, these Martian meteorites reveal what elements make up that planet.

When it comes to studying these rad rocks, Meenakshi Wadhwa has the (meteo)rite stuff. She's the director of the Center for Meteorite Studies at Arizona State University in Arizona, U.S.A., and an expert on meteorites that come from Mars. Studying them gives Wadhwa and other scientists clues about what the red planet was like when it was more like Earth—wet and warm. (Today, Mars is a huge, cold desert.)

During her studies, Wadhwa examined part of a meteorite called Black Beauty, which was found in the Sahara in 2011. At 4.4 billion years old, it's the oldest known hunk of Mars to land on Earth. It was formed after a volcanic eruption and contained traces of water. Wadhwa has also worked with NASA to study the data collected from samples of Mars rocks found by spacecraft that landed on the planet before InSight.

WHAT'S SHAKIN' ON MARS?

InSight is the eighth spacecraft that NASA has landed on Mars. For this mission, scientists from other countries, including France and Germany, helped out. InSight landed successfully on November 26, 2018, after a flight that took almost seven months and covered 300 million miles (483 million km). That's like taking more than 600 round trips to the moon!

Unlike past missions to Mars, this one is meant to measure any marsquakes that might take place. Like Earth, the red planet has seismic activity underground. Studying the quakes could help reveal what the inside of Mars is like. And that could help explain how Earth and other rocky planets formed. InSight recorded its first quake on Mars in April 2019.

Mars and Earth formed about 4.6 billion years ago. But why did Earth develop life whereas Mars didn't (as far as we know)? InSight could provide some answers. Among its tools is a device that can measure seismic activity. The spacecraft also has a probe that tried to drill where no Martian spacecraft has gone before: almost 16 feet (5 m) below the planet's surface to take its temperature. Not to see if it's sick, of course, but rather to detect how much heat is coming out of the inside of Mars. Unfortunately, the Martian soil proved a tough nut to crack, and the probe couldn't be buried beneath the surface.

UNDER THE SEA
• OCEAN COMMOTION •

PAY DIRT!

The valley along the Mid-Atlantic Ridge is up to 1.8 miles (3 km) deep—deeper than the Grand Canyon.

MID-ATLANTIC RIDGE

You're welcome!

Humans have studied the ground under our feet for many centuries. But it was only in the 1870s that scientists really got their feet wet, so to speak, exploring the ocean floor. Much later, Marie Tharp was one of the scientists who showed that this "floor" had plenty of bumps in it.

During the 1940s, women were not allowed on U.S. oceangoing research vessels. But Tharp took the data collected on those ships and used her scientific smarts to create a map of the bottom of the Atlantic Ocean. She and her partner, Bruce Heezen, discovered that a long mountain chain sat in the middle of the ocean floor and that along the center of these mountains was a deep valley, or rift. They went on to show that a single underwater mountain chain went all around the globe. Tharp also supposed that new crust pushed through the ocean bottom to create the nearby valley. Further research showed that underwater earthquakes often happened along this valley. As other scientists looked at the maps Tharp and Heezen made, they saw that continental drift was real. Their work helped others develop the theory of plate tectonics.

MASSIVE MOUNTAINS

Since Tharp made her discovery more than half a century ago, scientists have learned much more about the underwater peaks. The mountains under the Atlantic and other peaks like them around the globe are called mid-ocean ridges. Altogether, there are 40,000 miles (64,374 km) of these mountains, and 90 percent of them are completely underwater, some as much as 13,100 feet (4,000 m) below the ocean's surface. The ridges appear where two tectonic plates separate. The plates at the Mid-Atlantic Ridge separate at a rate of about .75 inch (2 cm) a year—about as fast as your fingernails grow!

The mid-ocean ridges also contain active volcanoes, and they play a key role in creating new crust for Earth. When the volcanoes erupt, their lava creates new oceanic crust. The movement of Earth's plates also "recycles" old oceanic crust. Where plates converge, or come together, old oceanic crust sinks into the mantle, where it melts. This magma might then return to Earth's surface in a volcanic eruption.

THAT'S SMOKIN'!

When new crust forms on the ocean floor, some very cold water flows down into it through cracks along the top of underwater volcanoes. The extreme heat below the crust heats the water to superhigh levels—up to about 750°F (400°C). This hot water then shoots back out through the seafloor. It looks like black smoke, but it's actually water filled with elements such as zinc, copper, and sulfur. As hot water from the vent hits the cold ocean water, the elements form minerals and create what look like small chimneys. Scientists call the spots where this hot, dark water erupts hydrothermal vents. The vents are also often called black smokers. Sea creatures found nowhere else on Earth survive around the black smokers, including giant tube worms up to 12 feet (4 m) long!

WHERE IN THE WORLD?
PROTECTING AN UNDERWATER WONDER

Some of the underwater volcanoes eventually stop erupting and form what are called seamounts. Off the coast of the United States, several seamounts are part of the country's first marine national monument in the Atlantic Ocean, designated by President Barack Obama in 2016. Northeast Canyons and Seamounts National Monument, which encompasses 4,913 square miles (12,725 sq km) has three canyons deeper than the Grand Canyon and four seamounts that are home to many kinds of sea life, including endangered and threatened species such as sperm whales and Kemp's ridley sea turtles.

IGNEOUS ROCKS
• HOT STUFF •

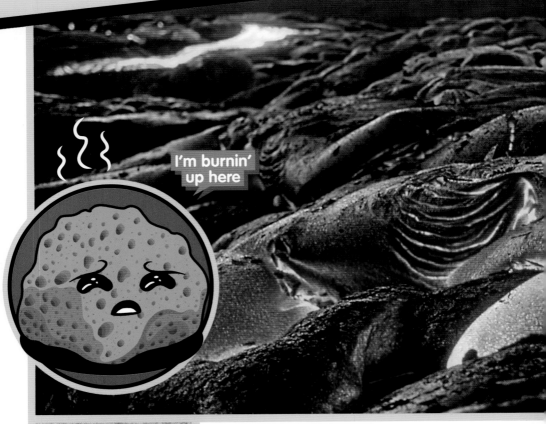

I'm burnin' up here

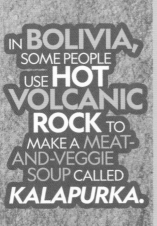

IN **BOLIVIA,** SOME PEOPLE USE **HOT VOLCANIC ROCK** TO MAKE A MEAT-AND-VEGGIE SOUP CALLED **KALAPURKA.**

Before they take a solid shape, igneous rocks start as hot, bubbling magma way deep beneath us. How hot is hot? The molten rock in Earth's crust and upper mantle can be more than 2000°F (1093°C)! That's hot enough to turn a gold ring into a puddle of metal.

Magma forms when rocks in the lower part of Earth's crust and the mantle melt. There are also radioactive elements, such as uranium, present in the crust and mantle that give off intense heat. The heat, combined with the pressure way below the surface, turns rocks into this molten material. When magma reaches the surface after flowing up through cracks in the crust, it makes a volcanic eruption. The magma is then called lava.

COOLING DOWN

Some rocks underground become liquid magma. Some magma becomes lava, and when this lava cools, it creates one of the two types of igneous rocks. Most of the crust on Earth is made up of these rocks. They form when lava cools quickly above the ground and are called volcanic, or extrusive, igneous rocks.

But some magma never breaks through Earth's surface. It cools off slowly underground, over thousands or even millions of years, forming intrusive igneous rocks. This long cooling process gives these rocks much larger crystals than their extrusive counterparts. Intrusive rocks appear on the surface only after they have been pushed up by tectonic forces or after erosion wears away the rocks that sit above them.

DIAMOND VOLCANOES

Not all volcanic eruptions are created equal—some can shoot diamonds to Earth's surface! Gases underground, such as carbon dioxide, come under extreme pressure and push a type of intrusive igneous rock called kimberlite through the mantle and crust and onto the surface. The kimberlite forms what's called a pipe. This pipe is shaped a little like a carrot—narrow at the bottom way belowground, and much wider at the surface. As the rock rushes upward through the carrot, it carries along different minerals, including diamonds. These diamonds go for quite a ride: When kimberlites plow through to the surface, they can reach speeds of more than 150 miles an hour (240 km/h).

WHAT'S IN A NAME?

Intrusive igneous rocks are also called plutons. The word comes from Pluto, the Roman god of the underworld.

I am so honored

DID YOU KNOW? THE FLOATING CLEANER

You might have cleaned your hands with rocks and not even known it. An extrusive igneous rock called pumice is an ingredient in one type of soap, and the stones themselves can be used to make rough skin soft again. Another weird thing about pumice: It's the only rock that floats! It's filled with tiny holes formed from gas bubbles that were trapped in the rock when it cooled.

GRANITE
• HARD ROCK •

I was built to last

BY THE NUMBERS

The Great Pyramid's **2.3 MILLION** stone blocks are estimated to weigh an average of **2.5 TO 15 TONS** (2.3 to 14 t) each!

It's easy to take granite for granted. Humans have been turning granite into various items for thousands of years, from ax heads to sculptures. Granite is the most common intrusive igneous rock in Earth's crust, making up about 70 percent of the planet's continents.

Granite is made up of three main minerals: feldspar, quartz, and mica. These and other minerals give most granite a light color—usually gray, white, or pink. Some rocks are called black granite. But even though they are intrusive igneous rocks, they are not true granite. Huge stretches of granite, up to several hundred miles long and hundreds of feet high, can appear on Earth's surface, even as the rock also extends deep into the ground.

A ROCK THAT LASTS

People sometimes compare things—or even people!—to blocks of granite, to show that they're hard and strong. Granite's toughness and ability to support a lot of weight have made it a popular building material since the days of the ancient Egyptians. They buried their rulers, called pharaohs, in huge pyramid-shaped tombs using granite and carved statues depicting the pharaohs out of the rock, too.

The Great Pyramid, built for the pharaoh Khufu circa 2550 B.C., is made of granite and limestone. Amazingly, the workers who constructed the pyramids managed to get the granite from a quarry hundreds of miles away—most likely by pulling the large stones from the quarry using ropes and a type of wooden sled, or perhaps by rolling the stones using wooden poles. Then, the workers put the granite on boats that sailed close to the building site.

During the 18th century, a single slab of granite weighing more than 1,500 tons (1,361 t) was used as the base for a statue in St. Petersburg, Russia, called the Bronze Horseman. It's thought to be the largest single stone ever moved from one place to another.

Today, you're likely to still see granite as a building material. It's used on the outside of buildings, in monuments, and as kitchen countertops.

DID YOU KNOW?
GRANITE WONDERS

Yosemite National Park, in California, U.S.A., is the site of some of the most spectacular rock formations made of granite in the world. Over millions of years, rivers and glaciers eroded rocks around the granite, exposing such sites as the wall called El Capitan. Soaring almost 3,000 feet (914 m), El Capitan is one of the largest exposed granite monoliths in the world.

IN 2017, ALEX HONNOLD BECAME THE FIRST PERSON TO FREE SOLO EL CAPITAN, MAKING THE CLIMB WITHOUT A ROPE OR SAFETY GEAR.

ROCK OF AGES GRANITE QUARRY, VERMONT, U.S.A.

WHAT'S IN A NAME?

Huge areas of granite are called batholiths. The name comes from the ancient Greek words *báthos*, meaning "depth," and *lith*, meaning "rock."

25

GRANITE AROUND THE WORLD

• A GREAT GRANITE TOUR •

Grab your passport! We're taking a quick trip around the world to see some of the most awe-inspiring buildings and impressive art that feature granite.

MOUNT RUSHMORE

Heads up! The heads of U.S. presidents George Washington, Thomas Jefferson, Theodore Roosevelt, and Abraham Lincoln—each about 60 feet (18 m) tall—were carved out of a South Dakota, U.S.A., granite batholith that began to form more than one billion years ago. Some of the faces have fractures in them, so the National Park Service uses sensors to detect if any of the granite has moved. So far, none has, but who knows what these faces will face in the future.

BRIHADISVARA TEMPLE

One thousand years ago, a king built this temple in Thanjavur, India, to honor the Hindu god Shiva. His workers constructed it entirely from granite—no easy feat, since there was no granite near the site! It's believed that workers used a boat to bring the granite—more than 100,000 tons (90,718 t) of it!—from a quarry about 30 miles (50 km) away. At the top of the temple's central tower, more than 200 feet (61 m) high, sits a single piece of granite that weighs about 80 tons (73 t).

BUNKER HILL MONUMENT

When it comes to history, Boston, Massachusetts, U.S.A., really rocks. The city's Bunker Hill Monument marks the site of a key battle at the start of the American Revolution in 1775. Planning for the monument began in 1823, and the 221-foot (67-m)-tall granite tower, called an obelisk, was completed in 1842. The granite came from a quarry in the nearby town of Quincy, after traveling on one of the first railways built in the United States. It was soon called the Granite Railway, and the rocks rolled along the track on cars pulled by horses, not steam engines.

TOWER BRIDGE

This is one London bridge that won't be falling down anytime soon. The Tower Bridge is one of the most famous sites in the United Kingdom's capital city. Its roadway is in two sections that lift to let large ships pass through. While its basic structure is made of 11,000 tons (9,980 t) of steel, the bridge also contains 31 million granite blocks that cover part of the outside.

27

BASALT

• PASS THE BASALT, PLEASE •

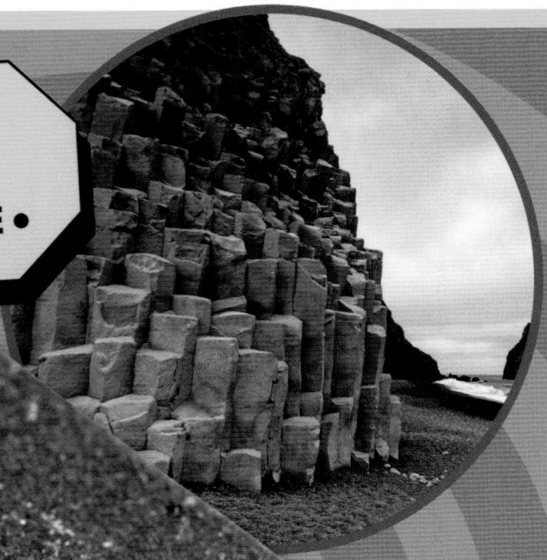

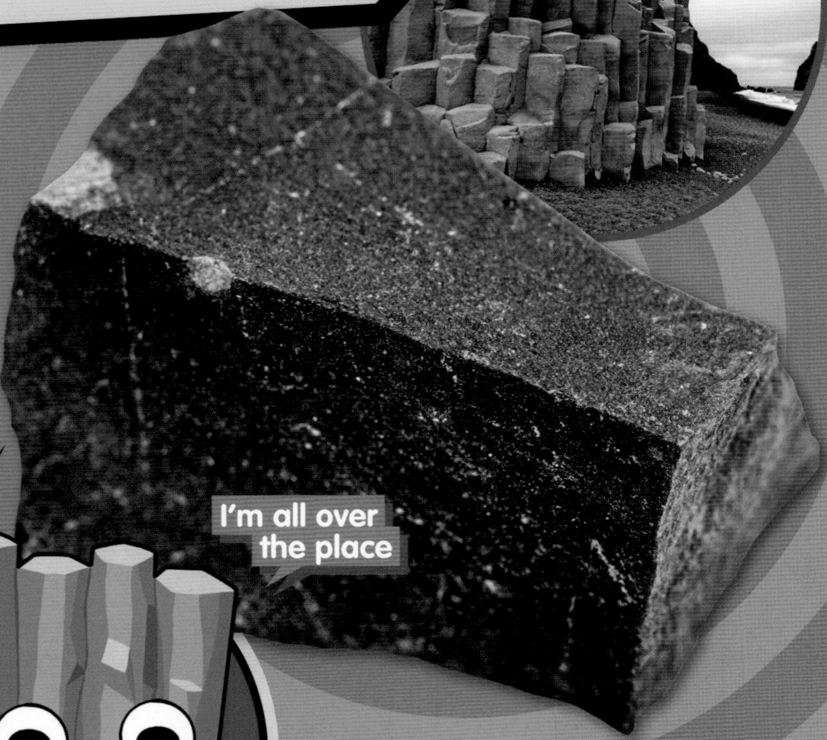

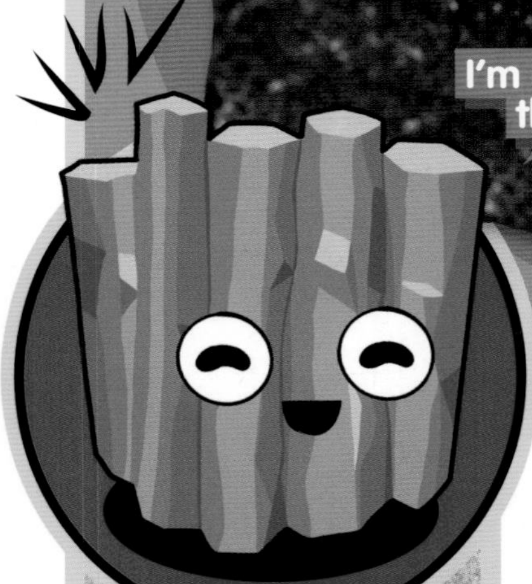

I'm all over the place

If you want to know rock basics, you've got to know basalt. It's not only the most common extrusive igneous rock, it's also the most common rock on Earth. It makes up most of the crust under the planet's oceans. On land, ancient volcanic eruptions left behind molten trails of basalt that hardened and now stretch out for miles. Iceland, which has lots of volcanoes, is bursting with basalt from both old and new eruptions.

Some basalt also reaches Earth's surface in the middle of tectonic plates through cracks called fissures. The molten lava spreads out in what scientists call a flood basalt. One of the largest of the flood basalts took place about 250 million years ago in a part of Russia called Siberia. This slow seeping of the molten basalt may have also released gases that killed off many of the animals then living on Earth.

SVARTIFOSS (BLACK WATERFALL), ICELAND

THE MOON ON EARTH

Hawaii, U.S.A., and the moon have something in common. No, not tropical breezes: a bonanza of basalt. The Hawaiian Islands are made up largely of this igneous rock, which came from volcanic eruptions that began about 30 million years ago. The basalt there is like the moon's, so studying the rocks in Hawaii could help prepare for future trips to the moon. Scientists are exploring how to make building materials out of Hawaiian basalt, so that moon settlers could use the same methods to make materials there. A lunar lifestyle could be based on basalt!

BASALT-Y SEAS

You won't just find basalt under your feet—if you look up at the sky, you can see it on the moon, too! Those dark patches dotting the surface are from lava flows that came from volcanic eruptions several billion years ago. Early astronomers thought the dark spots were water, and they called them seas. The astronauts of Apollo 11—the first humans to walk on the moon—landed on a spot composed of basalt called the Sea of Tranquility. Two Italian stargazers first named the area almost 400 years ago.

PUTTING BASALT TO GOOD USE

Our early ancestors used basalt to make tools as many as three million years ago. In more recent times, the Aztec of what today is Mexico created a huge, round stone carving out of basalt. Known as the Sun Stone, it was carved from a single chunk of basalt that weighed 25 tons (23 t). Basalt has also been used to make buildings, such as the temples at Ellora Caves in India. The 34 caves were cut out of basalt cliffs starting 2,000 years ago.

WHERE IN THE WORLD? STEPPING STONES AT SEA

In County Antrim, on the coast of Northern Ireland, there are about 40,000 columns of basalt known as the Giant's Causeway. Legend has it that a giant Irish warrior named Finn McCool threw huge pieces of the rocky coast into the sea, and some stories say he used the columns to walk all the way to Scotland.

VOLCANOES
• ALL FIRED UP •

VOLCÁN DE FUEGO, GUATEMALA

et's take a dive into the source of basalt and many other igneous rocks by exploring volcanoes. A volcano is an opening in Earth's crust where magma erupts onto the surface. At that point, it's called lava. Along with the lava, a volcano can also shoot out ash and gases.

Not all volcanoes are alike, as you'll soon see. Ones that have erupted within the past 10,000 years or so are called active. Dormant volcanoes are resting—they haven't erupted during that time frame but could come to life again. And extinct volcanoes are the quiet ones in the bunch. Their erupting days are done.

RED-HOT ROCKS

At times during eruptions, clumps of red-hot lava harden as they fly through the air, turning into "volcanic bombs." These rock bombs can travel more than 3,000 feet (914 m), and they're so hot that they can start fires. They can be big, too. One bomb that shot out of a German volcano weighed about 130 tons (118 t).

CONES, SHIELDS, AND DOMES

Cones filled with ice cream can be a great treat, but here are some cones you won't want to eat! Many volcanoes have a cone shape. Cinder cone volcanoes form from eruptions of mostly ash, not lava. Bits of the ash build up over time to create the cone-shaped volcano. One cinder cone volcano, Paricutín, in Mexico, first formed and began erupting in a cornfield in 1943 and destroyed a village of the same name. Composite cone volcanoes are made from a combination of ash and lava. At 14,410 feet (4,392 m) tall, Mount Rainier, in Washington State, U.S.A., is an example of a composite cone volcano.

Another type of volcano is called a shield volcano. Some people say this wide and flat volcano looks like an ancient warrior's shield lying face up on the ground. These volcanoes form from thin lava that moves easily over the ground, spreading out far from the eruption site. Much of Hawaii, U.S.A., is made up of the tops of shield volcanoes that dot the floor in that part of the Pacific Ocean.

Unlike other volcanoes, lava domes do not usually have raging flows of lava. Instead, their lava is thick and sticks close to the vent, or hole, that produced the magma. Mount St. Helens, another volcano in Washington State, had a large lava dome develop in it before it erupted in 1980.

BY THE NUMBERS
VOLCANOES

- Active volcanoes on land worldwide: **ABOUT 1,500**
- Active volcanoes in the United States: **ABOUT 170**
- Total underwater volcanoes, all kinds: **UP TO 1 MILLION**
- Highest active volcano: Nevados Ojos del Salado, along the Chile-Argentina border, **22,563 FEET** (6,877 m)
- Height of the dormant **MAUNA KEA** volcano in Hawaii: Measured from its base in the ocean, it's more than **33,000 FEET** (10,058 m) tall, making it the tallest mountain in the world.

WHAT'S IN A NAME?

Devils Tower is made of a kind of rock called phonolite, which comes from Greek words that mean "sounding stone." Some people say that when this rock is struck with a hammer, it makes a ringing sound.

WHERE IN THE WORLD?
A LOTTA LAVA

You don't have to enter an evil underworld to see Devils Tower, a huge pillar that rises 867 feet (264 m) above the land in northeastern Wyoming. This U.S. national monument was created from magma that pushed up into sedimentary rock tens of millions of years ago. Over time, the surrounding rock eroded away, leaving behind the igneous tower.

VOLCANOLOGISTS
• DIGGING DEEPER INTO VOLCANOES •

ARIANNA SOLDATI STANDING ON FRESH LAVA, GUATEMALA

WHAT'S IN A NAME?

"Volcano" comes from Vulcano, the name of a volcanic island off the coast of Sicily. Ancient Romans believed their god of fire, named Vulcan, lived there.

If you want to know what's bubbling in the world of volcanoes, ask an expert—a volcanologist. These geologists specialize in the study of volcanoes and their eruptions. Some try to give us a heads up when a volcano is about to erupt. Others study the many volcanoes on the ocean floor.

Becoming a volcanologist takes years of study—and the ability to stay cool when things get hot! Many volcanologists work near volcanoes just before or after they erupt and are often the first people to see lava begin to harden into new rock. Volcanologist Arianna Soldati says that most people think of volcanoes as forces of destruction, but she says they are also the source of new land—for example, in recent decades the Big Island of Hawaii has grown by hundreds of acres courtesy of eruptions at Kilauea volcano. And the morning coffee many grown-ups guzzle may have come from beans grown in Hawaii's rich volcanic soil.

SAFE SCIENCE

Soldati is a lava lover, and she's one of the scientists who can stand the heat. Most volcanologists, she says, don't need to wear those special flame-resistant silvery suits, which are just too heavy to wear while trekking miles to a volcano. But the experts do wear sturdy boots, thick gloves, a hard hat, and safety goggles. And because most volcanic gases are deadly, the volcanologists sometimes need a gas mask.

Lava and gases aren't the only dangers the scientists face during a day at their outdoor "office." When lava bombs shoot out, they can hit scientists before they see them coming. In recent decades, several scientists have died while working around volcanoes that were still erupting. Flying above active volcanoes to study them can be risky, too, as the clouds of ash that fill the air can clog airplane and helicopter mechanisms. Some dangers don't come from above—in Alaska, U.S.A., some volcanologists have had close encounters with bears!

PAY DIRT!

Volcanologists say an eruption in western Utah, U.S.A., some 30 million years ago was one of the largest ever, leaving lava deposits more than two miles (3.2 km) thick.

SOLDATI SITTING ON A LAVA BOMB

GEYSERS & MINERAL SPRINGS

• THE HEAT IS ON •

Thar she blows

GEYSER ERUPTION, ICELAND

PAY DIRT!

Geysers are unpredictable: Steamboat Geyser in Yellowstone National Park once went 50 years without erupting. From 2018 to 2020, however, it erupted more than 100 times!

Magma isn't the only hot stuff under Earth's surface. Geysers—columns of scorching hot water—shoot through holes and cracks into the air, propelled by intense pressure and heat underground. Geysers are just the most awesome example of what geologists call hydrothermal features. *Hydrothermal* refers to hot water from inside Earth.

Some people say the best way to put a spring in your step is to head to a hot spring. A soak in the mineral-rich waters is said to help treat all sorts of ailments, including arthritis and asthma. At minimum, the hot waters can soothe sore muscles and help you relax.

Hot springs occur in many spots in the southwestern United States. One town known for its healing waters is Truth or Consequences, New Mexico, U.S.A. (Yes, you read that right.) Some of the waters there contain more than 30 minerals, including tiny amounts of gold, silver, and copper, with temperatures ranging from 98° to 115°F (37° to 46°C). And about the town's odd name: It used to be called—not surprisingly—Hot Springs. But in 1949, a radio show called *Truth or Consequences* said it would broadcast from any city that changed its name to the name of the show. The people of Hot Springs voted to change their name, and it has been Truth or Consequences ever since. The locals call it T or C. But it's the mineral water, not the funny name, that draws people to the town.

IT'S ALL IN THE PLUMBING

Hydrothermal events start when water from rain and snow passes through rocks and soil and collects underground. If that happens where magma is close to the surface, the water gets hot. It then returns to the surface, where it usually collects in pools. These pools are called hot springs. But sometimes, the structure of the rocks underground doesn't allow the hot water to flow easily to the surface. Instead, steam from the hot water builds up, until the pressure is so high it forces hot water out of vents in the ground. It's almost like when a pipe springs a leak. Except, instead of flooding a basement, water shoots up dozens or hundreds of feet into the air.

A MINERAL MAKER

When a geyser blows, more than water comes to the surface. Chemical compounds such as silica and calcium carbonate are in the water, and they often collect on the ground, forming minerals near where the water erupts and lands. The silica creates a mineral called geyserite.

WHERE IN THE WORLD? HYDROTHERMAL HEAVEN

OLD FAITHFUL GEYSER

If you've got a hankering for hot water, head to Yellowstone National Park. Located in the U.S. states of Montana, Idaho, and Wyoming, the park has more than 10,000 hydrothermal features, including more than 500 geysers. That's more geysers than at any other location on the planet!

The Yellowstone geyser called Steamboat doesn't erupt often, but when it does, it's a record setter. With water blasts between 300 and 400 feet (91 and 122 m) high, it's the world's tallest geyser. By contrast, another of the park's geysers, Old Faithful, goes off once about every one to two hours. What sparks all the hydrothermal activity at Yellowstone? The park sits on top of a lot of magma. Some of it is just three to eight miles (5 to 13 km) below ground.

OBSIDIAN
• GLASS WITH CLASS •

WHAT'S IN A NAME?

The ancient Roman historian Pliny the Elder said a man named Obsius first discovered obsidian, leading to its name.

Obsidian is an extrusive igneous rock. It's often black, but it can come in a wide range of colors. A natural form of glass, it has a smooth, glassy surface and is formed by lava that cools very rapidly after erupting from a volcano. This quick cooldown keeps crystals from forming, and that gives obsidian its shiny look.

A GLASS ACT

Of all the ancient peoples who found uses for obsidian, the Aztec were a cut above. Along with using the rock to make spearheads and arrowheads, they put many small obsidian blades on a piece of wood to create a *macuahuitl*. A warrior swinging one of these "swords" could really do some damage to an enemy—even cut off their head! Although obsidian is sharp, it breaks easily, so a warrior would have to replace the macuahuitl's blades fairly often. But the volcanic glass wasn't just used for warfare. The Aztec also used obsidian to make knives for cutting cotton and feathers, and they polished it to make mirrors.

AN OBSIDIAN VASE MADE BY THE AZTEC

GETTING TO THE POINT

Like manufactured glass, if you break a piece of obsidian, its edges are sharp—sharp enough to use as a weapon or blade. This made the rock a valuable resource in ancient times. More than 15,000 years ago, people in parts of Turkey started to gather some obsidian they found and traded it with people in the Middle East, including what is now Iraq. The obsidian "miners" in Turkey might have received food or other items in return. Native peoples in North America also traded obsidian, sometimes exchanging it with other groups from hundreds of miles away. Some rulers liked the look of the smooth, shiny stone, so they used it for jewelry instead of turning it into tools.

OBSIDIAN CAN BE SO SHARP—**SHARPER THAN STEEL,** EVEN—THAT **SOME SURGEONS** HAVE USED **OBSIDIAN BLADES** TO PERFORM OPERATIONS.

This won't hurt a bit!

WHERE IN THE WORLD? GO WITH THE FLOW

In Deschutes National Forest in Oregon, U.S.A., you can stroll along a flow of obsidian. The Big Obsidian Flow also features pumice (see page 23), another igneous rock produced when Newberry Volcano let loose about 1,300 years ago. The volcano is still active, and U.S. government scientists watch it closely to try to learn when it might erupt again.

TUFF
• EXPLOSIVE STUFF •

It's not too tough to understand: Tuff is an extrusive igneous rock that forms with a blast. Some volcanoes produce lava that simply flows down their sides. But others have explosive eruptions that shoot out hot ash, lava, and pieces of rock. Together, this volcanic mixture is called tephra. If the tephra is hot enough when it lands, it fuses together to form tuff.

A ROCK "STEW"

The different bits of material from a volcanic eruption can range in size from tiny particles of ash to rocks as big as a boulder. The size of the different particles helps geologists classify different kinds of tuff. Some is made mostly of ash, while some is made up largely of pieces of rock called blocks and bombs, which are at least 2.5 inches (6.4 cm) across. Some tuff also contains bits of volcanic glass. Tuff often is found near a volcano's vent, and different layers of the stuff often build up over time. Each layer comes from a different eruption. Over the centuries, people living near volcanoes have often used tuff to construct their homes and other buildings.

ITALY'S TUFF TOWNS

The people of Pitigliano, Italy, and nearby villages didn't just make a building or two out of tuff. Pitigliano itself sits on tuff cliffs, and parts of it were carved out of the volcanic rock. Starting more than 2,000 years ago, the first settlers to the region carved tunnels out of the tuff from their hilltop homes down to their farmland below. Tuff building blocks were used to construct castles and churches—some of which are still standing. But the years have been hard on the soft rock. Landslides and erosion from wind and rain can send buildings sliding down the slopes. By 2004, about 10 percent of the village of Sorano had disappeared. In Civita di Bagnoregio, tourists pay a small fee to explore the tuff town. The money pays for efforts to reinforce the tuff cliffs so they don't slide away.

PAY DIRT!

Rapa Nui (also known as Easter Island), about 2,000 miles (3,220 km) off the coast of Chile, has three major volcanoes and several smaller ones. Many of the famous stone heads on the island, called moai, are made of tuff and weigh up to 80 tons (73 t).

WHERE IN THE WORLD?
TUFF TO BEAT

What may have been the largest explosive volcanic eruption in history took place in the San Juan Mountains in southwestern Colorado, U.S.A., some 27 million years ago. And when the dust settled, the eruption left behind one giant trail of tuff. The Fish Canyon Tuff, near Creede, Colorado, formed as a moving flow of ash turned solid. Before turning solid, the ash had a volume of about 1,200 cubic miles (5,000 cubic km)—roughly the volume of Lake Michigan. That makes Fish Canyon one of the world's largest ash flows.

GEODES
• COVERT CRYSTALS •

Large deposits of tuff and other igneous rocks can sometimes hold one of the coolest items in the world of rocks—geodes! From the outside, geodes don't look like much—just dark rocks that are often round, though they can be other shapes as well. But the real wonder of geodes comes when you crack one open, almost like a rock egg.

JOURNEY TO THE CENTER OF THE GEODE

Geodes are hollow, and their insides can be lined with glistening crystals that can come in a rainbow of colors. Most geodes start out as a gas bubble trapped inside cooling lava. The lava hardens around the bubble as the gases slowly seep out of the lava, leaving a hole in the center of the newly formed rock. Then, over thousands or even millions of years, water filled with minerals flows through tiny holes in the rocky shell. The minerals form the crystals inside the rock that make geodes so prized by rock collectors around the world. Different minerals leave behind crystals of different colors.

• GORGEOUS GEODES •

GIANT GEODES

Amethyst geodes are often long and thin and maybe a little pointy—like the top of a church. That's given them the name cathedral geodes ... and they can be big! This amethyst geode is about 12 feet (3.7 m) tall and is on display in New York City's American Museum of Natural History. Discovered in Uruguay, its history goes back to a volcanic eruption some 135 million years ago!

GREAT AGATE

Sometimes the hole in the lava gets completely filled with minerals, in which case it's no longer called a geode. Instead, it's called a nodule. The mineral agate often fills these solid centers. Other materials in the water that carry the agate help create the colorful bands that make agate nodules so popular. Once the nodule is split, some people polish the surface and use the agate as jewelry or colorful bookends.

THE SURPRISE INSIDE

For people who want to crack open their own geodes, some museums and stores sell small geodes like these. At home, the geode seekers carefully split open the rock to reveal the crystals inside. They never know what they'll find.

PUTTING GEODES TO GOOD USE

Not all geodes form in igneous rock. Some also form in sedimentary rocks, such as limestone (see page 50) or shale (see page 56). A U.S. region that stretches from eastern Iowa to Kentucky and Tennessee is famous for its sedimentary geodes. In some areas, the geodes are so plentiful that people have used them for building structures. Local geodes in Jasper, Indiana, were used to construct a spiritual site called the Mother of God Grotto.

BY THUNDER

Here's an egg you won't want on your plate. A thunder egg is like a geode, but it forms in a particular type of lava flow that's high in the mineral quartz. Thunder eggs are common in Oregon, U.S.A., and Native Americans there gave the rock its name. The Warm Springs people believe that two mountain gods sometimes got angry with each other. As thunder shook the area, the gods went to battle by hurling the "eggs" at each other, some of which landed near the tribal members' homes. Today, the thunder egg is Oregon's state rock.

ROCK HOMES
• HOME, ROCK HOME •

Every critter needs a home of its own, and for some of them, rocks are the answer. These rocky homes can be on mountainsides, in forests, deep underwater, or in caves. They may not be big—no room to throw parties in these places!—but the rock abodes provide safe spots to sleep and eat. Here's a look at just some of the wildlife that call rocks their home.

If looks could quill

1 ALL RIGHTY, DEN

If you wander along the cliffs of Washington State's Columbia National Wildlife Refuge, you might see "doorways" to several animals' homes. Porcupines, bats, and woodrats are just some of the mammals that seek shelter in holes along the basalt cliffs or under rocks. Sometimes you can tell what animal lives in what hole by the smell outside the home—a skunk's hole in the rocks is hard to miss! For porcupines, rock piles provide a den where they can safely spend the winter. In some parts of the United States, as many as 100 porcupines have been found sharing one rock pile.

② GOING DEEP

Nematodes are tough. Just how tough? These worms can survive where many other living things would never set foot, like in hot springs that reach 142°F (61°C) or in frozen Antarctica—even inside other animals! Nematodes can also live in rocks more than two miles (3.2 km) underground. (That's deeper than any other creature has ever been found, other than microscopic bacteria.) Scientists found the worms in a South African gold mine, living in water that collects in holes that had been drilled by geologists years before. The nematodes feed on millions of bacteria that clump together into a sticky gel that forms near holes in the rock. So, the worms can thank geologists for giving them a place to dine and live.

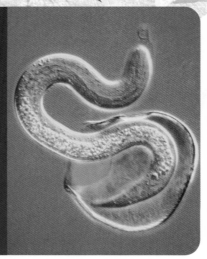

③ A "CHEWSY" SEA CREATURE

Step on a sea urchin and you might end up with one of its pointy spines in your foot. But the spines aren't the only sharp part of some sea urchins. Their teeth are sharp, too—sharp enough to drill through rock! Sea urchins like to hide out underwater in holes in rocks—holes they make themselves by scraping the rock to get their food. And they're not just able to gnaw through soft rock, like basalt. Scientists studying sea urchins in a lab found they can also chew through granite—one of the world's hardest rocks. Amazingly, chomping through rock doesn't dull an urchin's teeth. Instead, the ends of its teeth break off, exposing another sharp edge underneath. How much rock can a sea urchin eat in a day? About as much as the weight of three pennies. Not much, maybe, but for a person to eat the same amount of rock, depending on his or her weight, that could mean eating five pounds (2.3 kg) of the hard stuff! And that's the tooth!

④ IN THE SOUP!

Speaking of unusual things to eat, some people in Asia consider bird's nest soup quite a delicacy. But not just any nests work for this recipe. The ones people prize are made by swiftlets that build their nests into the limestone walls of the Gomantong Caves in Sabah, Malaysia, on the island of Borneo. For several centuries, local people have climbed up bamboo ladders and onto platforms to pry the swiftlets' nests off the walls. The Gomantong Caves are also the home of other creatures, including bats and cockroaches that feed on the waste the birds and bats produce. That waste is powerful stuff—it produces an acid that eats away at the caves' rock walls, just like water can erode rocks outside the cave.

SEDIMENTARY ROCKS
• THE MAIN SQUEEZE •

LAYERS OF SEDIMENTARY ROCK, UTAH, U.S.A.

A **RAINDROP** CAN CREATE WHAT'S CALLED **SPLASH EROSION**, HITTING **PARTICLES OF SAND** AND SHOOTING THEM UP TO **TWO FEET** (0.6 M) **AWAY.**

Sedimentary rocks are the second of the three major rock groups. The word comes from *sediment*, which refers to pieces of rock that break off existing rocks. You'd have to try really hard not to find a sedimentary rock near where you live. About 80 percent of Earth's land surface is covered with them!

You could call sedimentary rocks Earth's recycling project. Most of these rocks start to form when igneous, metamorphic, or other sedimentary rocks break down due to weathering. The sediment is carried by the wind, water, or glaciers to new locations—much of it ending up at the bottom of rivers or lakes.

As sediment piles up, the bits at the bottom get squished together from the weight on top of them. And minerals carried by water are like a glue that binds together the sediment. Over millions of years, this pressing and "gluing" of sediment creates a new sedimentary rock. The rock forms in layers, called strata, as new deposits of sediment land on existing ones. Rocks formed this way are called clastic sedimentary rocks, and they're the most common type.

Some sedimentary rocks form from ancient plants or sea creatures—or what's left of them, anyway. These biologic sedimentary rocks commonly come from the shells of tiny, dead sea creatures, such as clams.

Other sedimentary rocks form when water carrying minerals collects in a pool and then dries out. These deposits are called evaporites.

WONDERFUL WATER

Water plays an enormous role in the creation of rocks. In the form of rain, it weathers sedimentary rocks. Rain can also carry away bits of this sediment to bodies of water—rivers and streams transport sediment to lakes and oceans. The moving water in streams can erode rocks, too, creating more sediment. And if water gets inside cracks in rock and freezes, then melts and freezes again, the rock can start to break apart, creating more sediment. The tiny pieces are then whisked away by more water.

I'm feeling sedimental

WHERE IN THE WORLD?
IT'S A (SAND) BLAST

Want to see a stone "tree"? Head to the Eduardo Avaroa Andean Fauna National Reserve in Bolivia. The formations here show the power of natural forces to wear away rock over time, as the wind picks up sand that weathers the larger stone. A stone that has been eroded by windblown sand is called a ventifact.

45

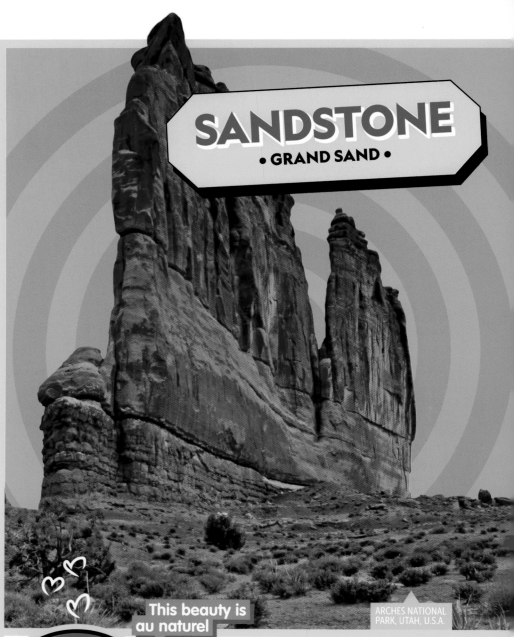

SANDSTONE

• GRAND SAND •

This beauty is au naturel

ARCHES NATIONAL PARK, UTAH, U.S.A.

Whether you're exploring the desert in the Southwest United States or strolling down a city street, you're likely to come across sandstone. It's one of the most common sedimentary rocks, and it's been used to construct buildings all over the world. During the late 1800s, many of the stone buildings in New York City were made of brownstone, a form of sandstone. And here's a grave fact about sandstone: It's often the material used to create headstones in cemeteries.

The "sand" in sandstone might conjure up a picture of a sunny beach, but you probably wouldn't want to stretch out on a patch of this hard rock. "Sand" actually refers to the size of the grains found in it. These grains can be tiny pieces of rocks and minerals, such as quartz, mica, feldspar, and basalt, or even the remains of plants and animals that lived millions of years ago.

STICKING TOGETHER

Holding together the sand-size pieces are other minerals that act like cement. These minerals include silica, calcium carbonate, and iron oxide. Sandstone packed with silica is often used to make glass.

The color of the minerals in sandstone creates rocks of different hues. Iron oxide, for example, gives sandstone a reddish look. Greensands refers to a type of sandstone that turned green from the mineral glauconite.

PAY DIRT!

The original White House in Washington, D.C., U.S.A., was built out of local sandstone that was then whitewashed. The famous residence was later rebuilt after it was damaged by fire in 1814 during the War of 1812.

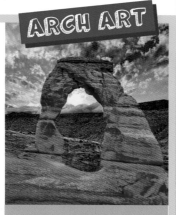

ARCH ART

Head to Arches National Park in Utah, U.S.A., and you'll see sandstone "sculptures" created by nature. The park has more than 2,000 natural stone arches shaped by wind and water that range in size from approximately three feet (0.9 m) to more than 300 feet (91 m) across.

About 300 million years ago, the park was covered by an ancient ocean. After this ocean dried up, it left layers of sedimentary rock more than a mile (1.6 km) thick covering the area. Over time, forces inside Earth uplifted the area and erosion by water and wind wore away that rock, creating the arches we see today. The park also has huge sandstone rocks that sit on thin "necks" of rocks. In some spots, it looks as if you could stomp your feet and send a big rock crashing down! One of these balanced rocks, called, fittingly, Balanced Rock, weighs about 3,600 tons (3,266 t). Over time, the base holding it up will erode, and the rock will take a tumble.

WHERE IN THE WORLD?
RAINBOW ON THE GROUND

Some of the sandstone mountains in China's Zhangye Danxia Geological Park in Gansu Province are "painted" every color of the rainbow. Millions of years ago, two tectonic plates smashed together in this part of Asia, turning flat land into a mountain range. That crash exposed rock that had been underground. Then, water eroded the mountains, exposing stripes created by different minerals in the rocks.

GLACIERS
• NICE ICE •

I missed my ride!

HUBBARD GLACIER, ALASKA, U.S.A.

How do some grains of rocks and minerals move from one spot to another? They hitch a ride on huge mounds of moving ice called glaciers. But the trip is nothing like zooming along on an express train. Glaciers move very slowly. Some barely move at all, and the fastest travel only about 150 feet (46 m) a day. Even a snail, the slowpoke of the garden, can go faster. So now you know why people sometimes say things that move slowly go at a glacial pace.

Why meeee?

GRASSHOPPER GLACIER IN MONTANA, U.S.A., IS **FILLED** WITH **MILLIONS** OF **FROZEN LOCUSTS** THAT GOT CAUGHT IN A **STORM** MORE THAN **200 YEARS AGO.**

MAKING A GLACIER

Glaciers form in cold regions as snow piles up and doesn't melt. Over decades, the pressure from new snow turns the bottom layers of snow into ice. As the weight of the snowpack builds up, gravity causes it to slowly move downhill.

Glaciers can form in what seem like unlikely spots. In Africa, Tanzania's Mount Kilimanjaro is near the Equator, but the mountaintop gets enough snow to have glaciers. Near Earth's North and South Poles, glaciers form on flat land, too, covering wide areas. These ice sheets can be several miles thick.

ICE MEETS ROCK

Glaciers are some of the most masterful sculptors in nature—their movement carves away some of the land underneath them. This has created valleys in many of the world's mountainous regions. As glaciers move, they carry along bits of rocks that form new sedimentary rocks—sometimes transporting them for hundreds of miles.

A glacier is always moving forward. But when it melts faster than the rate it's moving, its front edge will move back, or retreat. When a glacier retreats, it leaves behind a mixture of rocks, mud, and gravel called till. The stones and rocks found in till are called erratics.

A PEAK SPOT

Let's get right to the point—some mountains have peaks called horns, and they can thank glaciers for that. These pointy peaks occur where three or more glaciers met and eroded the rocks. One of the most famous of these peaks is the Matterhorn. Located in the Alps, it sits on the border between Italy and Switzerland. Most of the mountain is made up of sedimentary rock, but the top part is metamorphic rock that was once part of Africa. Did it vacation in the Alps and decide to stay? Nope—some 45 million years ago, a piece of a tectonic plate that was once in Africa broke and collided with a European plate. The collision brought a bit of Africa to the Alps.

WHERE IN THE WORLD?
ONE BIG BOULDER

The erratics that glaciers leave behind can be as small as pebbles or as big as boulders. Okotoks, a town near Alberta, Canada, is the home of the world's biggest erratic. The "Big Rock," as it's called, is some 30 feet (9 m) tall, 135 feet (41 m) long, and 59 feet (18 m) wide. The giant erratic weighs 16,500 tons (15,000 t)— just a little more than the combined average weight of 8,200 cars!

BIG ROCK, ALBERTA, CANADA

LIMESTONE
• A WATERY ROCK •

But where's the lime tho?

Limestone often forms in warm, shallow waters that were once home to ancient shellfish. The shells of some creatures contain either the mineral calcite or aragonite, which are both made from calcium carbonate. Pieces of ancient shell settled on the ocean bottom, and, over time, they turned into limestone. The water itself may also have calcium carbonate in it. Changes in water temperature make the mineral precipitate, or turn into solid particles. These particles then bind together to form limestone.

While limestone has watery roots, today you can find it far from an ocean—like on the top of Mount Everest. The world's highest mountain has limestone that formed hundreds of millions of years ago on what was a sea floor. Thanks to the movement of tectonic plates, that rock slowly got pushed upward. During the 20th century, geologists discovered the remains of ancient sea creatures in Everest's limestone. That was one of the clues the scientists followed to develop the theory of plate tectonics.

STICKING WITH IT

Heating limestone creates a substance called quick lime, a key ingredient that ancient Romans used to create long-lasting concrete. It's so durable that 2,000 years later some of the building material is still holding strong in Italian harbors. Meanwhile, modern concrete, which usually contains limestone, can crumble after just 50 years of use. What's the secret to the tougher Roman stuff? Scientists announced in 2017 that the Romans' combination of lime, volcanic ash and rock, and seawater created two superstrong minerals that strengthened the original concrete. And as more seawater seeped into the installed concrete, more of the minerals formed, making the concrete stronger over time.

PAY DIRT!

Madagascar's Tsingy de Bemaraha National Park is covered with limestone "needles" that provide shelter for many animal species found nowhere else in the world.

WHERE IN THE WORLD? LIMESTONE FLAPJACK STACKS

You won't find anything to eat when you visit these massive pancakes in New Zealand. That's because the flapjack-looking stacks at Paparoa National Park in Punakaiki are actually made of rock. The limestone here formed about 30 million years ago underwater, then got boosted up to the surface thanks to earthquakes. After all that, wind and water eroded the limestone to form what look like pancakes. The site is also famous for its blowholes—spots where water from the ocean rolls in and shoots up through gaps in the rocks. When the water erupts, it looks a little like a whale spouting water through its blowhole.

LIMESTONE STRUCTURES
• PUTTING LIMESTONE TO GOOD USE •

Limestone ends up in many different products—from paint to calcium supplements. It is also an important construction material, and not just as an ingredient in cement. Some of the world's most famous structures are made completely or mostly out of limestone. Here's a look at some of them.

STEPPING UP

When the Spanish invaded Central America during the 16th century, they came upon the Maya city of Chichén Itzá in what is now Yucatán Peninsula in Mexico. One of the most impressive buildings there was the Temple of Kukulkan, which the Spanish named El Castillo—"the castle." This stepped pyramid is like a stone calendar, as it has 365 steps, one for each day of the year. It and many other buildings in the city are made from limestone, which the Maya cut using simple stone tools made from flint or obsidian. To get the construction really rolling, workers pushed the limestone blocks to building sites by rolling them on logs.

CARVING OUT HISTORY

This desert statue featuring a lion with man's head was carved out of a single piece of limestone. That's no small feat: The Great Sphinx of Egypt is 66 feet (20 m) tall and 240 feet (73 m) long, and each of its paws is as long as a bus! No one knows exactly when the likeness of this mythical creature was carved, but it's more than 4,000 years old. The head may be an image of the Egyptian pharaoh Khafre. His dad, Khufu, built another of Egypt's famous rock structures: the Great Pyramid.

STATELY SKYSCRAPER

When the Empire State Building in New York City was completed in 1931, it was the tallest building in the world. The 1,250-foot (381-m) skyscraper features more than 200,000 cubic feet (5,663 cubic m) of limestone and granite that came from a quarry in Indiana, U.S.A. The limestone and granite, along with brick, went over a steel frame. The Indiana limestone is fairly soft when it comes out of the ground, but it hardens as it dries out. Similar limestone was used to construct several other famous buildings in the Big Apple, including Rockefeller Center. That's where a giant Christmas tree is set up each year, drawing tourists from around the world.

Lime falling in love

PRESIDENTIAL DIGS

It might be the most famous address in the United States: 1600 Pennsylvania Avenue in Washington, D.C.—where U.S. presidents get their mail delivered. The first White House, completed in 1800, got its white color from a paint made from crushed limestone and beer that workers applied to sandstone blocks using brooms. Limestone appeared again at the White House in 1902. White limestone was used for part of the work done when President Theodore Roosevelt wanted the building spruced up. And when President Donald Trump had some work done on his new home in 2017, the builders used Indiana limestone for some of the White House's steps. Other monuments and buildings in the nation's capital, including the Lincoln Memorial, the National Cathedral, and Union Station, also feature limestone.

LEAN INTO IT

Here's a tip: Pisa's famous tower might not be a place to visit if you like your buildings straight. The Leaning Tower of Pisa is a freestanding bell tower that is part of the Italian city's cathedral. In the 12th century, workers used limestone for the basic structure, then covered it with marble. The only problem was, the tower was too heavy for the soft ground that surrounded it, and the tower started to tip even before it was finished. Over the centuries, the tower continued to lean, and for a time, the Italian government closed it to visitors. In 1990, engineers began trying to stop the lean, in part by leveling the soil underneath it. Their efforts helped move the tower slightly back toward the center.

PALATIAL RUINS

In the days of ancient Rome, it was good to be emperor. You could do pretty much whatever you wanted— like build a massive home that was both a palace and a fort. That's what Emperor Diocletian did at the beginning of the fourth century. His palace, in what is now Split, Croatia, featured marble and white limestone taken from the nearby island of Brac. By some reports, limestone from Brac was also used for part of the White House, though no one has found the records to prove it. Today, the renovated Diocletian's palace contains shops, restaurants, and apartments.

53

STALACTITES & STALAGMITES

• POINTING THINGS OUT •

WHAT'S IN A NAME?

Both "stalactite" and "stalagmite" come from the ancient Greek word *stalassein*, which means "to let drip."

CAVE WITH STALACTITES AND STALAGMITES

Rock on dudes!

SOME STALACTITES HAVE BEEN "GROWING" FOR MORE THAN 190,000 YEARS!

I f you ever wander into a cave carved out of limestone, take a peek overhead. Chances are, a sharp rock formation that looks like a giant icicle is pointing right at you. Other rocks that look like small towers might rise out of the cave floor. The rocky icicles are called stalactites, and the towers are stalagmites.

A MINERAL MIXTURE

What's nature's recipe for creating stalactites and stalagmites? Liquid, gas, and solid rock all play a part. Water passes through limestone and mixes with the gas carbon dioxide—the same gas that gives some soft drinks their bubbles. The combination of the gas and water creates a kind of acid that eats away at the limestone. This releases calcium carbonate into the water. Some of these mineral-filled drops of water drip from the cave's ceiling. As the water evaporates, calcite is left behind. More and more calcite collects in the same spot, creating stalactites.

For stalagmites, the water containing the calcium carbonite falls to the ground, and the water evaporates there. Slowly, a stalagmite starts to build. In some caves, a single stalactite and stalagmite might meet, forming what's called a column.

Finding it hard to tell the two rock formations apart? Here's some help: StalaCtites hang from the Ceiling, and stalaGmites form on the Ground.

SOME DEEP ROCK MUSIC

If you want to hear a really special rock concert, head to Luray Caverns in Virginia, U.S.A. The caverns hold what's been called the world's largest instrument— the Great Stalacpipe Organ. Pressing a key on the organ's keyboard causes a soft hammer to strike one of the 37 stalactites spread throughout the cave. The pointy "pipes" that make up this rock instrument cover some 3.5 acres (1.4 ha). Since the stalactites are struck to make their notes, the organ is really more like a bell or gong than a traditional pipe organ, which uses air to make sounds. But whatever you call it, the Luray Caverns stalactites rock out with some beautiful music.

WHERE IN THE WORLD? ONE HUGE HOLE

In 1991, when a Vietnamese farmer ducked into a cave to escape the rain, he didn't know he was making a major geological discovery. He had found the entrance to Hang Son Doong, one of the largest caves in the world. It's more than three miles (4.8 km) long, and in some spots it's 650 feet (198 m) high. One passage is so big that a huge commercial airplane could fly through it! The cave's name means "mountain river cave," and it was formed three million years ago by a river that plunged down a crack in limestone deposits in Vietnam's Quang Binh Province. Hang Son Doong opened for tourists to explore in 2013. In it, they see both stalactites and stalagmites. One of the stalagmites is more than 230 feet (70 m) tall—possibly the tallest in the world.

SHALE

• ALL HAIL, SHALE! •

I'm a little flaky

Shall we tell you about the most common sedimentary rock in the world? Well, we shall—it's shale. This rock is made up of mineral particles smaller than sand. It forms when slow-moving waters leave behind bits of clay and silt at the bottom of oceans and lakes and at places where rivers flooded. Over time, the grains pack down into layers of rock, and these layers make shale easy to break into flakes.

Pieces of shale are sometimes mixed with water to form a clay that can be used to make pottery. Clay made from shale also turns up in bricks, building

Shale we play?

WHERE IN THE WORLD?
BISTI WILDERNESS AREA

tiles, and cement. And if you're a tennis ace and have played on a clay court, you might have bounced a ball on bits of shale.

The Navajo of the American Southwest knew something about shale. They called one corner of their region Bisti (bis-TIE), which means "large area of shale hills." Today, Bisti refers to a wilderness area in the northwest corner of New Mexico. It formed as far back as 85 million years ago. Along with the shale hills are other rocks weathered over time to create a landscape that looks like something from another planet.

SHALE POWER

Shale comes in different shades, but some of the most important shale is black. It contains the fossils, or remains, of ancient plants and animals. Over millions of years, the remains of the living things that made the fossils turned into valuable natural resources—petroleum or natural gas, also known as fossil fuels. People use natural gas to heat homes and power the plants that generate electricity, and petroleum is the source of the fuel that powers cars and other vehicles. Other petroleum products turn up in a wide range of items—from basketballs to balloons.

CENTURIES AGO, **MONGOLIAN WARRIORS DIPPED** THEIR **ARROWHEADS IN OIL** FROM SHALE AND THEN **LIT THEM** ON FIRE TO CREATE **FLAMING ARROWS.**

LANDSLIDES
• SLIPPERY SLOPES •

Heads up!

Coming through!

LANDSLIDE AFTER HEAVY RAINS, FRANCE

A landslide is a kind of natural disaster in which rocks, dirt, mud, and other debris move down a slope. Shale is one of the rocks often associated with these natural disasters. Clay in the shale absorbs water, which makes the rock prone to slide. In some cases, rocks fall off steep cliffs, creating what are called rockfalls.

Landslides can start in many ways. Earthquakes can shake the rocks loose, and violent storms or volcanic eruptions can trigger a slide, too. So can erosion caused by streams and rivers. And human activity sometimes plays a part. Cutting out new roads or maintaining existing ones can let loose a stream of rocks.

CONTROLLING SLIDES

Landslides can move quickly, and they can be dangerous. Once a landslide starts, it can travel several miles, and some kinds of slides, called flows, reach speeds of 35 miles an hour (56 km/h). And like a rocky bulldozer, a landslide can push along anything that gets in its way—and roll right over homes. Some massive landslides have even destroyed whole villages. In a rockfall, if a huge boulder bounces out into a road, it can crush a car.

Luckily, engineers have devised some ways to reduce the risks of landslides and rockfalls. Protective netting can be placed over soil, or walls can be built to hold back a rock onslaught. In some cases, builders might blow up rocks that could be a danger in the future. And drainage ditches can stop water from making the soil soggy in the first place.

In the United States, many of the largest landslides have taken place in Washington State. One powerful landslide hit the state around the year 1450. Rocks and debris up to 400 feet (122 m) thick blocked part of the Columbia River, creating a natural land bridge. Local Native Americans called it the Bridge of the Gods. Washington experienced another huge landslide after the eruption of Mount St. Helens in 1980. It destroyed bridges and miles of roads, along with many buildings. In 1942, the completion of the Grand Coulee Dam on the Columbia River created Lake Roosevelt. In the years following, landslides into the lake sometimes created huge waves up to 60 feet (18 m) high. Some of these giant waves have destroyed docks along the shore.

THE **LARGEST** KNOWN **LANDSLIDE** TOOK PLACE ABOUT **10,000 YEARS AGO** IN WHAT IS TODAY **IRAN,** WITH ABOUT **55 BILLION TONS** (50 BILLION T) **OF ROCK** MOVING A DISTANCE OF ABOUT **NINE MILES** (14 KM).

CHALK
• THE WRITE STUFF •

5,000-YEAR-OLD ROCK ART, INDIA

Chalk it up to those ancient sea critters again—we wouldn't have chalk without them. Chalk is a sedimentary rock and a form of limestone that comes from the shells of tiny organisms, and much of it formed during what is called the Cretaceous period, which started about 145 million years ago. *Creta* is the Latin word for "chalk."

Tens of thousands of years ago, some of the world's first artists used chalk to draw on cave walls. Today, gymnasts get a grip with chalk: They use it to keep their hands dry before they do their routines. Chalk ends up in some fertilizers, too, which helps crops grow.

CHALK THAT IS USED TO WRITE ON BLACKBOARDS **ONCE CAME FROM** THE ROCK OF THAT NAME, BUT **TODAY MOST** OF IT **COMES FROM** THE **MINERAL GYPSUM** (SEE PAGE 137).

LIFE DURING THE "CHALKY" PERIOD

Chalk-late!? Where?

Perhaps the world's most famous chalk hills are the White Cliffs of Dover, on the south-east coast of England. In some spots, the cliffs reach 300 feet (91 m) high. For some English residents, these towering cliffs of chalk are more than pretty rocks. They are a symbol of their home-land. For centuries in the past, the white site was the last thing soldiers saw as they left to fight in Europe. For those who returned home, the cliffs were the first thing they spotted when reaching England.

PAY DIRT!

The Channel Tunnel, a tunnel beneath the English Channel between England and France, was partly dug through underwater deposits of chalk. Some of that chalk was moved to create a nature reserve in England.

Earth was a happening place when chalk was forming during the Cretaceous period. One of the ancient supercontinents, Pangaea, was breaking up, creating new continents. On land, dinosaurs of all sizes roamed the planet. Some of the most famous of that era were the three-horned *Triceratops*, the ferocious flesh-eating *Tyrannosaurus rex*, and the much smaller but equally frightening *Velociraptor*. The Cretaceous also saw an explosion of new flora around the world, including flowering plants. This period ended about 66 million years ago, and many of the plants and animals of the era were wiped out, likely when a giant asteroid crashed into Earth (see page 117). But the chalk that gives the period its name is still here today.

WHERE IN THE WORLD? CAVES CARVED FROM CHALK

Almost 3,000 years ago, people in the ancient towns of Maresha and Bet Guvrin, in what is today the nation of Israel, began dig-ging caves in the chalk that filled the region's hills. The rock was soft, so it was easy to dig, yet it was also durable. The peo-ple of Maresha and Bet Guvrin used the underground rooms and chambers lots of ways: to store food and water, bathe, press olives for oil, hide when enemies attacked, and bury their dead. About 3,500 of these chalk rooms still exist! Today, the caves are part of the Bet Guvrin National Park.

TUFA & TRAVERTINE

• TUFA THE PRICE OF ONE •

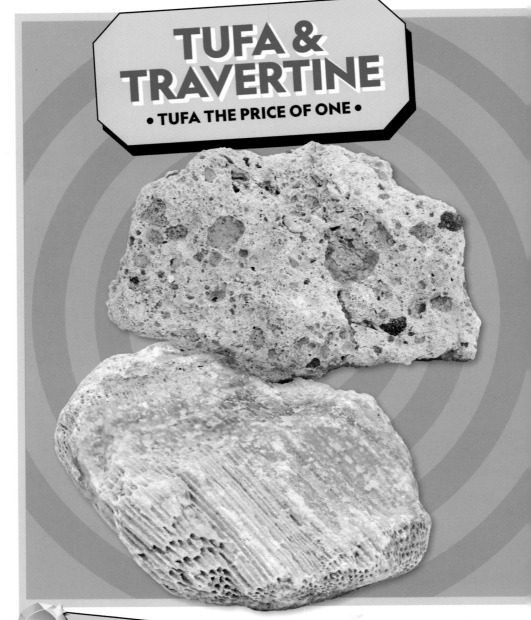

No, not tuba, tuna, or tofu—it's tufa! This sedimentary rock and another called travertine are both forms of limestone usually loaded with calcite. And tufa comes in twos, too. The type that is limestone and has calcite is the most common and is called calcareous tufa. A second form made from quartz is called siliceous tufa. Both tend to form around freshwater filled with either mineral, though tufa is usually found near cooler waters, while travertine is common around hot springs.

TURN TO STONE

When you're really frightened, you might freeze in place—one could say you're petrified. In nature, some things petrify, or turn to stone, thanks to a covering of tufa. At England's Petrifying Well in North Yorkshire, waters filled with calcite pour over a small waterfall. Hundreds of years ago, local people saw twigs and leaves in the water seemingly turn to stone, as tufa formed on them. They thought magic was at work, but today, we know it's simply chemistry that gives items in the water a stony covering. People place objects such as teddy bears in the water, and they petrify, too. It takes up to five months for a stuffed bear to petrify.

Tufa comes in odd shapes and is often filled with holes, while travertine is more solid. Both form as water evaporates and leaves calcite behind. The holes in tufa most likely come from plants or animals once trapped in the rock that then decomposed.

Both tufa and travertine can be used as building materials, with travertine sometimes used for tile. Ancient Romans used both travertine and tufa to build part of the colossal Colosseum, a giant outdoor arena. In more recent times, builders used Italian travertine—16,000 tons (14,515 t) of it!—to cover the outside of the Getty Center, an art museum in Los Angeles, California, U.S.A. Tufa has also become popular with gardeners, as they grow plants in the rock's holes. Because of its holes, tufa is lightweight, making it easy to haul around a garden.

WHERE IN THE WORLD?
"COTTON" ROCKS

If you want to relax in hot springs surrounded by what looks like ice, head to Pamukkale, Turkey. The mineral-rich waters there have created white platforms made of travertine. People have been coming for soothing soaks in these travertine tubs for more than 2,000 years! The baths at Pamukkale are kept cottony white by fresh deposits of calcite in the water.

FLINT
• A STINT WITH FLINT •

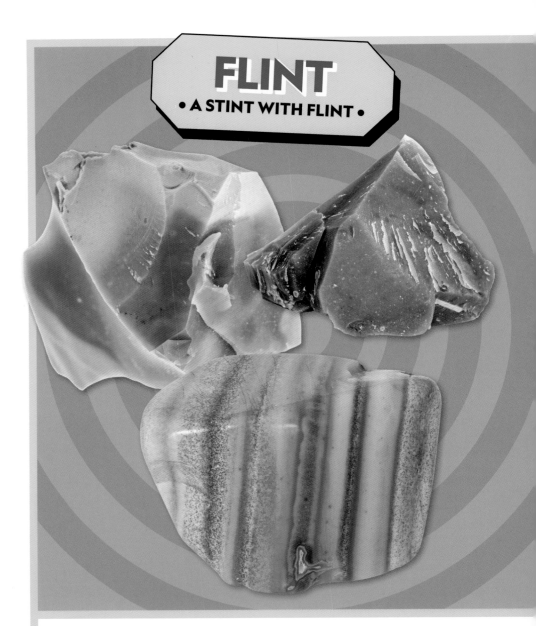

Ever heard someone described as flinty? That means they're hard and tough—just like flint. Like other sedimentary rocks, flint gets its start, in part, from the remains of ancient sea creatures. Their shells turn into the chemical compound silica, which dissolves in water and then re-forms as the mineral quartz.

Flint forms in round masses called nodules and often appears in chalk or limestone. It can also form in layers, and then it's usually called chert. Some people, though, call all examples of this hard rock "flint."

Need to light a fire? Flint can help do the trick. When it's struck against iron or steel, flint sends hot sparks flying. American soldiers used flintlock firearms in the 18th century during the Revolutionary War. Pulling the trigger on a flintlock weapon made the flint strike a piece of iron or steel. The spark that followed then made a small amount of gunpowder ignite, which then set off more gunpowder in the gun's barrel. When that powder ignited, it fired out a metal ball, called a shot.

TOUGH STUFF

Because flint is so hard, people have found many uses for it. The early ancestors of humans used flint to make tools about two million years ago. Later, people discovered that flaking off bits of a flint rock created a sharp edge, and so flint was used for the tips of arrows and spears. Flint's hardness also made it a good building material, since weather didn't wear it down. Hundreds of years ago, it was often used in parts of England to build churches, homes, and even some castles.

WHERE IN THE WORLD? GOING DEEP

More than 5,000 years ago, people living in what is today Norfolk, England, realized that they could find high-quality flint deep underground. Miners dug through approximately 30 feet (9 m) of chalk to get at the flint, and they kept working these mines for more than a thousand years. At a site called Grime's Graves, the miners dug about 400 different shafts. To make each one, they had to remove about 2,000 tons (1,814 t) of chalk—a job they did using deer antlers as their only tools! Each mine produced about 60 tons (54 t) of flint. The mining seemed to stop when the local people had access to bronze that they could use for weapons and tools. Today, tourists can climb down one of the mines at Grime's Graves.

THE STONE AGE
• ROCKY RESOURCES FOR AN ANCIENT AGE •

Nailed it!

WHAT'S IN A NAME?

The names for the three Stone Age periods come from Greek words meaning "old" (paleo), "middle" (meso), and "new" (neo), combined with the word for "stone" (lithos).

The Stone Age started at different times in different parts of the world, depending on when early humans first realized a rock could be a hammer or a weapon. The earliest known stone tools were made from volcanic rock more than three million years ago and were discovered near Lake Turkana, in Kenya. The Stone Age began to reach its end about 9,000 years ago, as people learned they could make better tools out of metal.

HANDY TOOLS

Historians usually break up the Stone Age into three periods: Paleolithic, Mesolithic, and Neolithic. Stone Age people of the Paleolithic generally made tools they could hold in their hands, like a sharpened stone to skin animals. Starting about 50,000 years ago, they also made handy tools called burins. With a small, sharp point on its end, a burin could be used for carving bones and other rocks to make new tools. Some of these new tools were the first needles, which allowed ancient people to begin sewing clothes. Paleolithic people in what is today Japan used microblades, and eventually, toward the end of the period, they began using clay to make pottery.

NEW AND IMPROVED

By the Mesolithic period, which began in some areas about 15,000 years ago, people were attaching sharpened stones to wood to make arrows and spears. Also during that period, stone tools called adzes helped early carpenters smooth and carve wood.

The Neolithic period started roughly 10,000 years ago, as people in different parts of the world began to raise crops for the first time. Stone workers began producing polished tools, and sharpened stone, such as flint, was used to cut down corn, not just foes on the battlefield. The corn was then sometimes ground for baking using stone discs. Thanks to stone tools and the spread of farming, the world's first towns began to develop.

A KNACK FOR KNAPPING

The process of shaping flint or other rocks to make tools is called flintknapping. Early toolmakers used animal bones or another hard rock to hit the flint. With each hit, a piece called a flake broke off. The flakes could then be whacked some more to shape them into arrowheads or scrapers. And flintknapping isn't just for Stone Age toolmakers. You can take classes in flintknapping today. An expert knapper can make a stone spearhead in about 20 minutes!

THE MUMMIFIED REMAINS OF A 5,300-YEAR-OLD MAN NAMED ÖTZI— ALONG WITH SOME OF HIS FLINT TOOLS— WERE FOUND PRESERVED IN ICE ON THE MOUNTAIN BORDER BETWEEN AUSTRIA AND ITALY IN 1991.

WHERE IN THE WORLD? STONE CIRCLE

One of the great structures of the Neolithic Age that's still standing is Stonehenge. The site in Salisbury, England, was first used as a cemetery about 5,000 years ago. Several centuries later, the local people began setting up huge slabs of sandstone called sarsen and different igneous rocks called bluestone. They arranged them in circles and arcs, with the larger sarsens on the outside. The largest of these stands about 30 feet (9 m) tall and may weigh 30 tons (27 t)! Some of the bluestones came from a quarry 140 miles (225 km) away. How Stonehenge's builders moved these and other massive stones to the site is one of history's great mysteries.

ARCHAEOLOGY
• UNEARTHING THE PAST •

I can dig it

AN ARCHAEOLOGIST STUDYING A 2,700-YEAR-OLD BURIAL MOUND, MONGOLIA

e know so much about Stone Age tools and how people lived long ago thanks to a special group of scientists who really dig history. Archaeologists sift through layers of soil and sediment to uncover items ancient peoples left behind. Most often, they find things made of flint or other hard, long-lasting materials, including animal bones, pieces of pottery, and charcoal from fire pits. Tools from organic sources, such as plants and animals, break apart over the centuries. Items made from rocks provide some of the best clues about what humans did thousands of years ago.

RECENT SECRETS

Some of the things archaeologists find are from the more recent past. In 2018, a team working in Australia announced a discovery after playing detective: The continent's first people, Aboriginal Australians, made tools of flint at the end of the 18th century. But around that time, there was no flint in the area around the city of Sydney, where the old tools were found. So where did it come from?

The archaeologists knew that the British had used flint pebbles as ballast—weight that helped keep their ships stable as they sailed. The ballast stones would be dumped overboard when the ships were loaded with goods to be brought back to England. Did the Aboriginal people pick up flint from the piles along the beach to use for their tools? Chemical analysis confirmed the hunch—flint found near London matched the flint in the tools. One rock history mystery solved!

HOW OLD IS THAT?

Through a process called radiocarbon dating, archaeologists can figure out how old an object or artifact is. Carbon is an element found in every living thing on Earth. One form of it, carbon-14, is radioactive. When a living thing dies, it stops getting carbon-14 from its environment. Scientists know that the carbon decays, or breaks down, at a certain rate. Knowing this, scientists can measure the amount of carbon-14 in the remains of a plant or animal and determine when it died, based on how much carbon-14 is still in it. Radiocarbon dating is useful for fossils and other organic materials (such as the charcoal from ancient fire pits) that are less than 60,000 years old. A similar process can measure the decay of other radioactive elements in rocks, revealing rocks more than two billion years old.

ROCK STAR THE CURIOUS COWBOY

After heavy rains hit Folsom, New Mexico, U.S.A., in 1908, George McJunkin rode his horse across the ranch where he worked to see whether the flooding had damaged any fences. Instead, McJunkin came across bison bones, but they were bigger than any bones of that kind he had ever seen before. A former enslaved person, McJunkin had taught himself how to read and was always interested in learning. Convinced the bones were very old and that he had made an important discovery, McJunkin contacted several scientists, but he never learned the true story of the bones. That information didn't come out until after his death, when archaeologists unearthed ancient spearheads from the same site where McJunkin had found the bones. Scientists determined that the flint spearheads were about 11,000 years old and that they had been used to kill the ancient animals whose bones had been found at the site. These spearheads were the first proof that humans had been living in North America for a lot longer than people thought. And cowboy George McJunkin rode into the history books.

METAMORPHIC ROCKS
• NO SMALL CHANGE •

METAMORPHIC ROCK FORMATIONS, SLOVAKIA

STRIKE UP THE BAND

Geologists classify metamorphic rocks into two major groups. With foliated rocks, the pressure that helped form them aligned their minerals into distinct bands or layers. Non-foliated rocks don't have bands. Slate is one example of a foliated rock, and marble is a well-known non-foliated rock.

If you say someone's "taking some heat" or is "under pressure," they're probably not feeling that great. But for metamorphic rocks, it's heat and pressure caused by volcanic and tectonic activity that make them what they are.

HEATIN' AND SQUEEZIN' AND MOVIN'

Deep underground, heat and pressure applied to igneous, sedimentary, and even other metamorphic rocks create new rocks. The pressure comes at places where tectonic plates move past or into each other or when rocky materials get buried deep underground. The heat comes from radioactive materials within Earth, the friction created by rocks moving past each other, or magma under the surface.

Geologists know that metamorphic rocks form in several different ways:

CONTACT METAMORPHISM: This refers to magma moving through Earth's crust and coming into contact with existing rocks. The intense heat from the molten rock creates chemical and physical changes in existing rocks, and new minerals form. New minerals mean new rocks. So, with contact metamorphism, the heat can turn sedimentary rocks like limestone and sandstone into marble or quartzite.

DYNAMIC METAMORPHISM: When you're dynamic, you're full of life and movement, and movement is the key to this process. Along faults in Earth's surface, rocks can grind together as tectonic plates move. This grinding creates some heat and a lot of pressure that turn the existing rocks into something new. Mylonite is one rock formed this way, and it can come from a variety of other rocks found along a fault.

REGIONAL METAMORPHISM: This process takes place over a large area, often where large continental plates come together and create mountains. This crashing of plates bends and twists the existing rocks to form new ones. The metamorphic rock slate is formed from the sedimentary rock shale, and, over time, the slate can transform into schist or gneiss.

WHAT'S IN A NAME?

"Metamorphic" is derived from the word "metamorphosis," which comes from two Greek words meaning to transform or change shape.

SOME METAMORPHIC ROCKS ARE **CAUSED BY EXTRATERRESTRIALS**—THEY **FORM FROM** THE **INTENSE HEAT** AND **PRESSURE** THAT HAPPEN WHEN A **METEORITE** CRASHES INTO **EARTH!**

MARBLE
• A FINE ART •

Call me
Captain Marble

Feeling fancy
and fine

Artists shape it, builders stack blocks of it, and some animals even eat it. You could say marble is a rock marvel! Marble is formed from limestone or dolomite. These two sedimentary rocks are a similar color and hardness, and both form in similar environments and have similar chemical compositions.

The main mineral in marble and its source rock is calcite. Heat and pressure within Earth change the calcite crystals. They start out small, but then they grow in size and lock together. That process makes marble much harder than limestone. Yet marble is also fairly easy to cut, as sculptors and builders have known for centuries. It can form in large masses hundreds of yards thick, and some quarries can produce millions of tons of marble in a single year.

FILLED WITH COLORS AND DESIGNS

Artists prize white marble for their work, as the way light reflects off it creates a creamy color. But marble can come in other shades, such as pink, green, brown, and black. It can also have patterns of darker colors mixed in with white—sort of like vanilla ice cream with chocolate swirls. The darker colors come from minerals in the original limestone. Some marble also has pieces of other rocks in it, creating what is called marble breccia. And from time to time, marble is studded with a valuable gem, such as a ruby.

NOT JUST A PRETTY ROCK

While people around the world admire marble's beauty, it has plenty of practical uses, too. Crushed marble is used in aggregate, a mixture of rock beneath railways and roads. Even tinier pieces of marble turn up in what's called whiting, a substance that gives some paints and paper a white color. Calcium from crushed marble sometimes ends up in feed given to chickens and cows.

SOME PEOPLE **PROTECT** THEIR **SMARTPHONES** WITH **CASES** MADE OUT OF **MARBLE.**

WHERE IN THE WORLD?
NATURE'S CHURCH

The Marble Cathedral is a name given to a series of caves carved out of rock at Lake General Carrera, the second-largest freshwater lake in South America. It sits on the border between Chile and Argentina in a region called Patagonia. Water created the caves, and silt from nearby glaciers gives the lake a distinct blue color.

MARBLE IN ART & ARCHITECTURE

• MAKING USE OF MARBLE •

Here's a look at some of the ways skilled sculptors and builders over the centuries have put marble to use.

1 THE TAJ MAHAL

The Taj Mahal in Agra, India, looks like a palace. Actually, it is a marble mausoleum (tomb) that holds the remains of Mumtaz Mahal, a wife of the emperor Shah Jahan, who ruled India nearly 400 years ago. Shah Jahan wanted to honor the memory of his late wife with this massive masterpiece.

The Taj Mahal is made from white marble that came from an area of India called Rajasthan. It features a marble dome 115 feet (35 m) tall, and gems were set into parts of the building. The site also has other buildings made from red sandstone. Finished in 1648, the Taj Mahal was constructed by 20,000 workers, including stonecutters, carvers, masons, painters, and calligraphers. Some 1,000 elephants were used to haul rocks to the site.

2 THE DAVID

My aim is marble-lous

You may know the biblical story of David and Goliath: The future king of Israel (David) fired a rock with his slingshot that killed the giant (Goliath). The story inspired the great Italian artist Michelangelo to carve this statue of David out of marble. Finished in 1504, the sculpture depicts David just before he unleashes his deadly stone. Michelangelo carved his marble masterpiece out of a single block of marble from a quarry in Carrara, Italy, located in mountains called the Apuan Alps. The region has been a source of fine marble for more than 2,000 years: Its marble was used to construct many buildings in ancient Rome. Today, Michelangelo's great statue is on display at the Accademia Gallery in Florence, Italy. With its precise detail, the David is considered one of the world's greatest works of art.

③ STATUE OF ABRAHAM LINCOLN

Steady as a rock

No trip to Washington, D.C., is complete without a stop at the Lincoln Memorial, which honors the 16th U.S. president, Abraham Lincoln. The central space inside features a marble statue of "Honest Abe" sitting down in a chair also made of marble. The 175-ton (159-t) statue was designed by American sculptor Daniel Chester French and carved by a family of famed Italian stone cutters, the Piccirillis, from 28 separate blocks that were carefully pieced back together when placed on the site. (The Piccirillis also crafted the marble lions that stand guard outside the New York Public Library.) The statue is 19 feet (5.8 m) tall, but if Abe could break free from the stone and stand, he would tower 28 feet (8.5 m) above his visitors.

④ BOCCA DELLA VERITÀ

No lie—this ancient marble face was thought to know whether or not people were telling the truth. The Bocca della Verità— the "Mouth of Truth"—is located at Santa Maria in Cosmedin, a church in Rome. The sculpture is 5.75 feet (1.75 m) wide and is thought to be the image of an ancient pagan god. According to legend, if someone stuck their hand into the marble mouth and told a lie, the face bit off their hand!

GNEISS

• GNEISS? NICE! •

Gneiss to meet ya!

WHAT'S IN A NAME?

"Gneiss" comes from the German word *gneis*, which means "spark." This refers to the pieces of quartz and mica in rock that sparkle.

This tough metamorphic rock has a gneiss name. (Get it? Because *gneiss* is pronounced like *nice!*) It can form from rocks in any of the three rock groups and is often found where two tectonic plates crash together to form mountains.

You could call gneiss the zebra of the rock world. The source rocks that turn into gneiss are usually loaded with the minerals quartz (see page 132) and feldspar. In gneiss, they show up as white bands. Meanwhile, other minerals, such as hornblende, create gneiss's darker stripes. Some stripes are wavy; others are straight. And some gneiss have large spots of feldspar that look like eyes. These rocks are called augen gneiss, from the German word for "eyes."

Gneiss-ly done

GNEISS WORK

Gneiss is one tough rock, which makes it perfect for practical use. For example, some "granite" kitchen countertops are actually made of gneiss. Along with preparing a meal on gneiss, you might walk all over it, as it's used as flooring. And graveyards may have gneiss headstones. You might not always see gneiss at work, though, since some of it is crushed and used under roads and building foundations.

When the ancient Egyptians wanted to honor the pharaoh Khafre, they chose gneiss for several statues of him. Khafre ruled about 4,500 years ago, and he was buried in a pyramid at Giza, near the Great Sphinx. The most famous statue of the pharaoh, which shows him sitting on a throne, was made of gneiss taken from a quarry in southern Egypt, where large boulders of the stone dotted the desert. The Egyptians also used gneiss to make stone bowls.

Thousands of years after Khafre lived and thousands of miles away, Americans used gneiss and other rocks to honor one of their own great leaders. The Washington Monument in Washington, D.C., which recognizes George Washington's military leadership during the American Revolution, is a 555-foot (169-m)-tall obelisk that includes blocks of gneiss in its foundation. The rocks came from a quarry in Maryland and were set in place in 1848. Construction on the monument took decades, and by the 1870s, engineers feared the original foundation would not support its weight. So in 1879, builders strengthened the foundation with more gneiss, sand, and cement. The monument was finally finished in 1884.

GNEISS IS SOME OF THE WORLD'S **OLDEST ROCK**—ONE **SAMPLE** FROM **CANADA** IS MORE THAN **FOUR BILLION YEARS** OLD!

WHERE IN THE WORLD? ICE AND GNEISS

Visitors to Rocky Mountain National Park in Colorado, U.S.A., find a landscape shaped by ancient glaciers. Some small glaciers still dot the park, which has a top elevation of more than 14,000 feet (4,267 m). Gneiss, along with granite and schist, is visible today in the park in some of the bowl-shaped areas carved out by past glaciers. The rock can also be seen while driving on Trail Ridge Road, which winds its way through the park for 48 miles (77 km).

FLORENCE BASCOM

• A ROCKIN' PIONEER •

ACADIA NATIONAL PARK, MAINE, U.S.A.

etamorphic rocks are all about change, and Florence Bascom made big changes in the world of science. She helped break down the barriers that kept women from studying geology and other fields.

A WOMAN OF FIRSTS

She earned bachelor's and master's degrees at the University of Wisconsin. When she earned her master's degree in geology, in 1887, the school had been letting women study there for only 12 years. In 1893, she became the first woman to earn a Ph.D. from Johns Hopkins University in Baltimore, Maryland. Soon after, Bascom became the first woman hired by the U.S. Geological Survey (USGS), and, in 1901, she was the first woman to present a paper at the Geological Society of Washington.

GETTING HER HANDS DIRTY

Starting at Johns Hopkins, Bascom headed out into the field to study and map rock formations in the northeastern United States. She became an expert in the geology of the Appalachian Mountains and helped map the rock formations there for the USGS. In addition, she was the first female professional geologist to study Mount Desert Island, the home of Acadia National Park in Maine, publishing a paper on its geology in 1919. In a report on her work, she noted the presence of all three groups of rocks and the effects of glaciers on the island.

Bascom also taught at several colleges. At Bryn Mawr, a women's college in Pennsylvania, she founded the geology department and played a key role in teaching other young women about earth science.

By the early 20th century, Bascom was recognized as one of the top geologists in the United States. She continued doing research into her 70s. Today, the Geological Society of America gives an award in her honor to geologists who carry out important mapping work.

ROCK STARS
EARTH TREK: THE NEXT GENERATION

Some of the female students Florence Bascom taught went on to become "rock stars" themselves:

ELEANORA FRANCES BLISS KNOPF: She earned a Ph.D. in geology at Bryn Mawr in 1912. She was a petrologist, which is a geologist who specializes in the study of rocks. Like Bascom, she spent many years working for the USGS and focused on the rocks of the northeast United States. With her geologist husband, Adolph, she also studied the Rocky Mountains. Knopf embraced new technology, such as pictures taken from airplanes that showed rock formations in 3D.

IDA OGILVIE: After she finished her studies at Bryn Mawr and then Columbia University, she taught geology at Barnard College in New York City for almost 40 years. Her research ran hot and cold—Ogilvie studied both volcanic activity and glaciers. Her work took her to some pretty spectacular spots, including Popocatépetl, an active volcano in Mexico. Along with her scholarly work in geology, Ogilvie was also famous for organizing young women to raise crops during World War I to help feed the country.

SLATE
• GREAT SLATE •

Look up and you might see slate covering a house's roof. Look down and it might be under your feet in an outdoor patio. Because slate is tough—able to withstand snow and rain and heat—it has been a popular building material for thousands of years.

This metamorphic rock can form from shale and mudstone, two sedimentary rocks, or from volcanic tuff that is rich in silica. Slate is usually dark and a little dull, but sometimes mica in the rock gives it a nice sparkle. The minerals in slate form in thin layers, which can be easily split off into thin sheets. That makes it ideal for turning slate into shingles. A slate roof can last hundreds of years, despite all the beating it takes from Mother Nature. And if one shingle does get damaged, it's easy to replace without tearing off the whole roof. But compared with other roofing materials, slate is expensive—too costly for the average home. One famous building with a slate roof is the Smithsonian Castle in Washington, D.C.

COMING CLEAN

The phrase "wiping the slate clean" means to make a fresh start with a project, especially if someone has made a mistake. In years past, though, it wasn't just a saying. American students really did wipe the slate clean to do their school work. Before paper and pencil were common in classrooms, each student had their own small piece of slate that they wrote on with a piece of soapstone or another rock. Taking notes on a tablet or smartphone is a lot easier, since you don't need an eraser when you make a mistake.

A WALE OF A ROCK

When the ancient Romans arrived in northern Wales around 2,000 years ago, they discovered the area was rich with slate. They used the local rock to build a fort and other buildings in a town known today as Caernarfon. The Romans didn't last in Wales, but the slate did, and over the centuries, mining it became a major industry. Welsh slate was used to build castles, and then it turned up in buildings in both England and North America. By the late 1800s, thousands of miners worked at the largest Welsh slate mines. Some slate from the region also ended up in pool tables! Chalk it up to the stone's smooth surface and toughness. Mining has left behind small mountains of slate waste—more than 700 million tons (635 t) of it!—but in recent years, a Welsh business has been recycling the waste into building tiles.

WHERE IN THE WORLD? SLATE CATHEDRAL

Many visitors to the province of Lugo, Spain, marvel at the natural beauty of Praia de Augas Santas, or the Beach of the Holy Waters. This shoreline wonder is also known as the Beach of the Cathedrals. Erosion has carved the slate and schist there into arches that look a little like some of the old, large churches found across Europe. At low tide, visitors can explore the arches and caves, but they have to be careful: High tide can come in quickly, covering both the rocks and tourists with water.

FULGURITE & TEKTITES
• THE SKY'S THE LIMIT •

TEKTITE

FULGURITE

WHAT'S IN A NAME?

"Fulgurite" comes from *fulgur*, the Latin word for "lightning," and "tektite" is derived from the Greek word *tēktos*, which means "molten."

ost of the heat that creates metamorphic rocks comes from deep within Earth. Sometimes, though, that powerful energy comes from above, like a bolt out of the blue—a lightning bolt, that is. Lighting is just some of the hot stuff that can turn one rock into another.

LIGHTNING UP

When a bolt of lightning flashes across the sky, it can heat the air around it to about 50,000°F (27,760°C)— five times hotter than the surface of the sun! Bolts that strike the ground are hot enough to melt the sand they hit, which then hardens into a new rock called fulgurite. These natural tubes or clumps of sand and rock are also referred to as "petrified lightning."

FULGURITE

What does a boy king wear? If you're a young Egyptian pharaoh named Tutankhamun—Tut to his pals—maybe a piece of gold armor with tektite in the center. It's believed that, more than 20 million years ago, something huge crashed in the desert of Libya, Egypt's neighbor to the west. That collision created tektites known today as Libyan desert glass. The stone was rare in Tut's time, and some of it was used to decorate a piece of gold armor called a breastplate. In 1922, scientists uncovered Tut's tomb and found the breastplate with the Libyan desert glass.

SMACKING DOWN

Heat from above also plays a role in creating an unusual rock called a tektite. As they crash into Earth, meteorites generate a lot of heat. This heat and the force of their impact can melt the rocks and sand they hit, forming little molten blobs that shoot off in all directions. These blobs cool into a glass-like substance—tektite. Many sources classify tektite as a contact metamorphic rock because an impacting meteorite produces a ton of heat and pressure. Since the material to make the tektite completely melted and then turned into a solid again, however, the case can be made to call it igneous. Whatever its classification, this rock is usually black and not very big, maybe the size of a peach pit, but some larger ones can weigh almost 30 pounds (14 kg). Tektites have been found on every continent except Antarctica. They're most common near sites where ancient meteorites left behind large craters, such as the Ries crater in Nördlingen, Germany.

Smashing!

WHERE IN THE WORLD?
FLORIDA'S FULGURITE

Florida is known for its sandy beaches, but you can find plenty of sand far from the shore. Sand mines in Polk County, in the center of the state, are the source of sand used to make cement and cover playgrounds. They're also a great place to find fulgurite—as Florida gets hit with more lightning strikes per square mile than any other U.S. state. At one Polk County mine, scientists found hundreds of examples of the metamorphic rock. And what's thought to be the longest fulgurite excavated in one piece was also formed in Florida: It split into three branches, one of which was 16 feet (5 m) long.

83

HORNFELS

• THE HEAT IS ON •

When things really get hot, some metamorphic rocks form just from heat—there's no pressure involved. Hornfels is one of these hot rocks. Intense heat from magma fuels the process that turns different "parent" rocks into hornfels. The "recipe" for making the new rock calls for baking the source rock at temperatures between 1300°F (704°C) and 1450°F (788°C).

The hot magma underground can turn a variety of parent rocks into newborn hornfels. Some of the more common source rocks are the sedimentary rocks sandstone and limestone, igneous rocks such as basalt and granite, and the metamorphic rock gneiss. Although hornfels can come from any of the rock types, it's most often found in layers close to Earth's surface near igneous rocks.

AN EARLY ROCK BAND

During the late 19th century, a group of musicians became famous for giving concerts in several countries that featured an instrument made of hornfels. The Till family from Keswick, England, used what they called a rock harmonicon. The harmonicon looked like today's xylophone, and similar instruments have been called lithophones. Pieces of the hornfels cut into different lengths made musical notes when the player struck them with a mallet. Before its metamorphosis, the hornfels was originally slate, and that rock was once mud that sat on an ancient ocean floor. The Tills weren't the first people to play these stone instruments. Similar ones using hornfels from an area in England called the Lake District date back to 1785. Some of the stone xylophones made from hornfels weighed about 1.5 tons (1.4 t). Talk about some heavy music!

WHERE IN THE WORLD?
STACKED MATS

In Japan, a tatami is a soft mat used to cover floors. But the Japanese also sometimes use the word "tatami" to describe a famous hornfels formation in Susa. This small village on the Sea of Japan is near Hagi, in the southwest part of the country. Light and dark layers of hornfels form cliffs about 50 feet (15 m) high that look a little like rock tatamis stacked on top of one another. The cliffs formed around 14 million years ago, as light sandstone and darker shale turned into hornfels.

FAMOUS ROCKS AROUND THE WORLD

• ROCKIN' THE GLOBE •

Some rocks stand out because of what they mean to people or cultures around the world.

SHIPROCK

What's a ship doing in the middle of a desert? Formed about 30 million years ago, this remarkable rock formation rises about 1,970 feet (600 m) above the surrounding land on the high desert plain of northwest New Mexico, U.S.A. Shiprock developed in the vent of an active volcano—becoming sort of like a cork in a bottle. The rest of the volcano eventually eroded away, leaving only this rocky "neck." Shiprock sits on tribal land of the Navajo Nation and is a sacred site to the Navajo people, who call it Tse Bitai—"winged rock." In one Navajo story, a giant winged monster lived on the rock, and two Navajo heroes killed it. Because Shiprock is sacred to the Navajo, visitors are not allowed to climb it.

PLYMOUTH ROCK

Not all famous rocks are as big as Uluru. But to the Pilgrims who landed in Plymouth, Massachusetts, U.S.A., in 1620, Plymouth Rock was still a big deal. Or so many people think. The Pilgrims who sailed from England on the *Mayflower* didn't note seeing a rock where they first landed. More than 120 years later, a local resident claimed that his father had heard from the early settlers that the rock *did* mark the spot where the Pilgrims had come ashore. The famous chunk of granite—deposited on Plymouth's coast by a glacier—is more than 600 million years old.

ROCK OF GIBRALTAR

If someone calls you their "Rock of Gibraltar," that's some high praise. It means they know they can count on you to help them through thick and thin. The real Rock of Gibraltar is pretty solid, too. Often called just "the Rock," it stands guard over the spot where the Mediterranean Sea and the Atlantic Ocean meet. Made of limestone and shale, the Rock—located on a tiny peninsula off of Spain—is just under 1,400 feet (427 m) tall at its peak. According to ancient Roman writers, the Greek strongman Hercules smashed a mountain that once linked Spain and Africa to create a waterway between them, resulting in the Rock.

ULURU

To the Anangu Aboriginal people of central Australia, Uluru is more than a massive rock. They believe it was created by their ancestors, and they hold different religious ceremonies there. The rock is made of a type of sandstone called arkose, which contains at least 25 percent of the mineral feldspar. Uluru is 1,142 feet (348 m) tall, and if you want to hike around it, bring plenty of water: It has a circumference of 5.8 miles (9.3 km)!

Magnificent like moi

You've already read about some animals that make their homes in and around rocks. But stone homes can be cozy for humans, too. Early humans and their ancestors often lived in caves, and some people still do. Here are some of the world's most famous rock homes.

1 PETRA, JORDAN

Forget about carving a home out of rock—the ancient inhabitants of Petra went for a whole city! Starting more than 2,000 years ago, settlers of the Nabataean empire began cutting into the red, white, and pink sandstone cliff faces surrounding a canyon called Siq, in the southwestern corner of what is today the country of Jordan. A thriving center of trade, the rock city had tombs, homes, and other structures, along with statues that lined the streets. Earthquakes destroyed many buildings, but several impressive ones still survive. The facade of the monument Al Khazneh ("the Treasury") was featured in the movie *Indiana Jones and the Last Crusade*.

2 CHACO CANYON, NEW MEXICO, U.S.A.

Looking for a home with some fine stonework? Check out Chaco Canyon. Starting about 1,200 years ago, ancestral Puebloans in what is now New Mexico lived across a large part of the Southwest. The community they built at Chaco Canyon had public buildings, homes, and religious sites and was larger than any other settlement in the region. The largest buildings are called great houses, and the largest of these is Pueblo Bonito. It has almost 650 rooms, and items found in a tomb there, including skeletons of tropical birds, show that the residents traded with people who lived hundreds of miles to the south. The buildings at Chaco were made out of sandstone, which surrounds the site.

4 GUYAJU CAVES IN CHINA

Tourists can visit a curious complex of some 117 caves chiseled into the side of a secluded gorge some 50 miles (80 km) northwest of Beijing, China. Though the caves are more than 1,000 years old, they feature surprisingly modern amenities, such as living rooms and beds that are heated using an ancient technology for funneling warm air. Experts believe the upper levels were mainly used by people while the lower levels housed animals. Rooms are connected by narrow passageways, and some you can descend into via stone ladders, forming an impressive maze-like structure. Although the creators of these caves left behind what some might consider a mountain of clues, archaeologists are still unsure exactly who built them.

3 DOGON VILLAGES OF AFRICA

In the African country of Mali, a people called the Dogon have built entire villages into sloping hills of sandstone called escarpments. Many Dogon live in homes carved into the cliffs, whose elevation traditionally helped protect them from enemies. It also helps keep the people cool, as the temperature is lower the higher you go. The escarpment area stretches for 95 miles (153 km) and is home to about 290 villages.

5 CAPPADOCIA, TURKEY

Some buildings have basement apartments, but in Cappadocia, Turkey, people really dug deep for their homes. The region features tons of tuff that formed from volcanic eruptions and was then carved by erosion into rock towers. Starting about 1,700 years ago, the first settlers of the area began digging into the rock, carving out tunnels and chambers that served as places of worship, storage spaces, homes—and even stables for horses! One of the many underground villages is Kaymaklı, which is eight floors deep. Another is Derinkuyu, which had 20,000 residents. The rock cities provided safety when enemies were nearby. The residents rolled rocks into the tunnel entrances to keep out their unwanted visitors.

ANCIENT ART
• A "CANVAS" OF ROCK •

PETROGLYPHS AT NEWSPAPER ROCK STATE HISTORIC MONUMENT, UTAH, U.S.A.

EXPERTS THINK THAT AN **ANCIENT ARTIST** AT CHAUVET CAVE **IN FRANCE** **SPIT RED PAINT** OVER A HUMAN HAND TO **LEAVE AN IMAGE** OF THE HAND ON A CAVE WALL.

When early cave dwellers wanted to spruce up their homes, they did what people do today—they put art on the walls. All over the world, ancient people drew on rock surfaces. Their paints were made with minerals of different colors. Red, for example, came from hematite, and a form of manganese was used to make black paint. Ancient artists ground or heated the minerals to prepare them before applying them to the walls.

MASTERPIECES FROM LONG AGO

Some of the greatest examples of cave art have been found in France, where people began living in limestone caves at least 36,000 years ago. In 1940, 18-year-old Marcel Ravidat and three friends found a cave in Lascaux, a site near the southwestern village of Montignac. Archaeologists soon discovered its artistic wonders: about 600 images painted on the

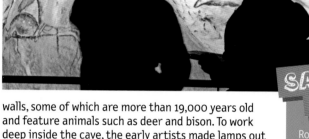

walls, some of which are more than 19,000 years old and feature animals such as deer and bison. To work deep inside the cave, the early artists made lamps out of sandstone. Clumps of lit animal fat sitting on the rock provided the flame.

As impressive as the Lascaux art is, another French cave revealed equally stunning rock paintings. The work at Chauvet Cave in southern France, discovered in 1994, is about twice as old as the images found at Lascaux. Some show woolly mammoths and other animals that died out thousands of years ago.

"CARVELOUS" WORKS

Not all ancient rock art involved painting. Some long-ago artists carved images into rocks, creating what are called petroglyphs. (Images painted on rocks, such as the cave drawings in France, are called pictographs.)

The rock carvers used two stone tools—one as a hammer and one as a chisel—to carve images of birds and animals. The art might also show shapes—circles or squiggly lines. Many thousands of examples of petroglyphs are found in the deserts of the American Southwest. The dry climate helps preserve the art on rocky cliffs.

SAVING CAVE ART

Rock walls can last a long time, but the art on them might not. The discovery of the Lascaux Cave drew thousands of people to admire the paintings there. Over time, an abundance of visitors negatively affected the air quality in the cave, and the images began to fade. As a result, officials restored the paintings and prohibited visitors to the cave.

After the discovery of Chauvet Cave, French officials prevented visitors from entering it. Instead, they built a model of the real cave in a concrete building. Using powerful computers and photographs, hundreds of artists and engineers re-created the Chauvet art. Since 2007, people have been able see what the ancient art looked like—without damaging the real thing.

WHERE IN THE WORLD?
ANCIENT ASIAN ART

In 2014, archaeologists dated cave art found outside Maros, Indonesia, to as far back as 40,000 years—comparable in age to the oldest European art. The find shows that early artists were scattered all over the world. Some scientists think there's even older cave art out there—they just have to find it!

FOSSILS
• OLD BONES IN STONE •

THE SCOOP ON ANCIENT POOP AND PUKE

By studying fossils, scientists can learn what ancient creatures looked like, how big they were, and sometimes, what they ate. Coprolites—a fancy name for poop that's turned to stone—and gastric pellets, also known as ancient vomit, offer valuable food clues. By studying one gastric pellet, for example, scientists were able to discover that the animal that had coughed it up liked to eat small lizards. And if coprolites contain bone fragments, scientists can deduce that the animal that it came from was a carnivore.

How do we know what living things existed on Earth hundreds of millions, or even billions, of years ago? The secrets are locked in rocks called fossils. A fossil is the preserved remains of any living thing. It can be a bone from a huge *Allosaurus* or the trace of the tiniest organism too small to see without a microscope. Footprints of ancient creatures are fossils, too. A plant or animal may have decayed long ago but left behind the outline of its shape in mud, volcanic ash, or sediment that eventually turned to stone. In rare cases, flesh and organs can be preserved, too. This happens with insects trapped in fossilized resin amber (see page 98) or tar and with animals that froze in ice.

A SPECIES OF **TRILOBITE—** A NOW **EXTINCT GROUP** OF MARINE INVERTEBRATES— WAS **NAMED**

HAN SOLO,

AFTER THE CHARACTER FROM THE **STAR WARS** **FILMS.**

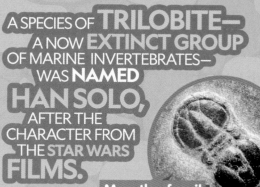

May the fossil be with you

FOSSIL FUNDAMENTALS

If someone called you spineless, you might get upset— it means they think you're not brave enough to do something. But when it comes to fossils, being spine-less is pretty common. Most fossils come from animals called invertebrates—those that don't have skeletons made of bone.

Many fossils are found in areas that were once ancient seas or lakes. When the organisms died, they were left in the mud. Over time, the water dried up, and the mud surrounding the creature turned to stone, producing the fossil. Often the original remains of the organism have decomposed, leaving an exact copy in the rock. Sea creatures with shells often have had their hard bodies preserved like this, too.

Fossils are almost always found in sedimentary rocks. Some types of limestone are made almost com-pletely of fossilized shells and skeletons from sea crea-tures. Fossils also turn up in sandstone and shale. The oldest fossils date back about four billion years and come from microscopic sea organisms.

BY THE NUMBERS
THE OLDEST OF THE OLD

Most of us like getting new things. But in the world of geology, the older something is the more prized it will be. Let's see just how old "old" can be.

- The oldest ice: **2.7 MILLION YEARS OLD**
- The oldest animal fossil: **558 MILLION YEARS OLD**
- The oldest volcanic lava flow: **3.8 BILLION YEARS OLD.** This lava flow was found during the early 2000s in the village of Inukjuak, in an area of Quebec, Canada, called Nunavik. There were probably earlier eruptions, however.
- The oldest mineral: **4.4 BILLION YEARS OLD**
- The age of Earth: **4.54 BILLION YEARS OLD,** well, give or take 50 million years.
- The oldest meteorite: **4.565 BILLION YEARS OLD**

DID YOU KNOW?
THE REAL DEAL

A rock formation called the Canadian Shield, in Nunavik, has granite that is believed to be part of Earth's original crust.

WHERE IN THE WORLD?
FOSSIL FINDS GALORE

Not all fossils are dug out of the rock that helped preserve them. Dinosaur National Monument near Jensen, Utah, U.S.A., has more than 1,500 fossils on display that are still in rock. They are some of the remains of about a dozen creatures, including the long-necked *Apatosaurus* and its contemporary *Stegosaurus*, known for the double row of plates running vertically along its back. The bones are preserved inside a building called the Quarry Exhibit Hall, and visitors can touch some of the fossils, which are as old as 149 million years.

PALEONTOLOGISTS

• BONING UP ON THE PAST •

Can you dig it?

Yes, I can

PALEONTOLOGIST WORKING WITH A RHINO FOSSIL, SPAIN

Sure—it's possible to stumble upon a fossil when you're out taking a walk. But to *really* uncover the secrets of ancient life, you often have to dig deep—and that's where paleontologists get their hands dirty. These scientists are trained to locate, unearth, and study fossils of all life-forms, from micro-scopic organisms to the biggest dinosaurs.

PUZZLING OVER THE PAST

Paleontology is a fairly modern science, dating from the 18th century, but some great thinkers of the past found fossils and had hunches about what they were. These early scientists also made good guesses about what the fossils meant for understanding Earth's history. One of the old-time smart guys was a Greek named Xenophanes. Around 2,500 years ago, he found a seashell on a mountain far from the shore. How had the shell gotten there? Xenophanes guessed that at one time the mountain was covered by an ocean. Other Greeks thought the ocean notion was kind of wacky, but Xenophanes was right. We now know that many parts of land were once covered by water, and these areas are often rich in fossils.

It took a long time after Xenophanes for paleontology to become a science. After him, people sometimes thought the fossils they found came from mythical beasts, like dragons. Others thought ancient bones were left behind by animals killed by the flood described in the Bible. By the end of the 18th century, though, scientists realized these ideas were all wet. Fossils come from real organisms that lived long ago. By studying fossils, paleontologists explain how humans and other living things evolved over millions of years.

Check it out

ROCK STAR
FANTASTIC FOSSIL FINDER

Making history when you're 12 years old is no easy feat, but around 1811, Mary Anning did just that. By then, she was already an experienced fossil hunter, a skill she had learned from her father. Together, they, along with Mary's brother, often searched for fossils on the shores of southwestern England, where they lived. Her first big find was helping to uncover the 17-foot (5.2-m)-long skeleton of an ancient sea reptile now called an *Ichthyosaurus*. Like many girls who lived during the early 1800s, Anning didn't have much schooling, but she could read. She taught herself geology and learned about the bones and bodies of different animals. And she didn't stop digging for fossils. Anning later discovered the first skeleton of a *Plesiosaurus*, another sea creature from the past. Male scientists at the time often did not give her credit for her work, but today Anning is considered one of the early heroes of paleontology.

HIGH-TECH TOOLS OF THE TRADE

Out in the field, paleontologists usually work with some pretty basic tools—hammers and chisels and brushes. But back in the lab, they often turn to technology to study their finds. In 2007, a reindeer herder in Siberia, Russia, found a complete fossil of a young woolly mammoth. (Mammoths are ancient relatives of elephants that have been extinct for about 4,000 years.) The bone-chilling cold of Siberia had preserved the creature's organs, as well as its bones. Paleontologists named their mammoth calf Lyuba and used a series of x-ray images taken from different angles to study her. The images revealed mud inside Lyuba's mouth and windpipe, suggesting to the scientists that the young mammoth had died by accidentally swallowing mud.

YOUNG PALEONTOLOGISTS

As Mary Anning showed 200 years ago, you don't have to be a scientist—or even be old enough to drive!—to find fossils. Here's a look at some other youngsters who uncovered bones to brag about.

THE DRAGON GIRL

When she was just three, Daisy Morris began searching for fossils on the beaches of England's Isle of Wight, where she lived. In 2008, when she was five, she found something black poking out of the sand that turned out to be some very old and very rare bones. Daisy's family took the bones to a paleontologist, who said they were fossils from a small flying reptile called a pterosaur, which lived more than 66 million years ago. Daisy's find, though, came from a type of pterosaur scientists hadn't known about before. In 2013, the new pterosaur was given the scientific name *Vectidracto daisymorrisae.* The first part of the name is Latin for "dragon from the Isle of Wight." The second part, of course, refers to the fossil's young discoverer.

BETTER THAN THE PROS

Professional fossil hunters should know what they're looking for, right? But sometimes even the experts walk right past important finds. That happened in 2009, leaving 17-year-old amateur Kevin Terris to make an important discovery. Terris was searching for bones in southern Utah, U.S.A., with two experts who had walked the same area a few days before. In a boulder, Terris spotted what expert eyes had missed: the fossil of a baby *Parasaurolophus,* a dinosaur that had roamed the region about 75 million years ago. The fossil Terris found is the most complete example of a young *Parasaurolophus* unearthed to date.

FROM HOBBY TO JOB

As a boy in northern England during the 1950s, Paul Taylor liked to walk along railroad tracks that ran through the region. On one jaunt when he was about 12, he came upon a heap of rocks and started digging through it. He pulled out some pieces shaped like darts or spearheads. They turned out to be what the British call thunderbolts—the name for fossils from creatures called belemnites. (The name thunderbolts came from the belief that lightning strikes formed them.) These are part of the remains of ancient relatives of squids that swam in the seas during the Jurassic and Cretaceous periods. Along with the belemnites, Taylor found other fossils that day in the rock pile. None of them helped him make the news—but they did stir his interest in learning more about fossils. Today, he is a professional paleontologist in London. He's even written a book about fossils for kids, so they can search for their own.

A LUCKY TUMBLE

Matthew Berger wasn't looking for fossils back in 2008. The nine-year-old was just chasing his dog Tau when he tripped over a log and saw some bones in front of him. The fossils turned out to be a shoulder bone and part of a jaw that belonged to an early ancestor of humans. How early? From about two million years ago! On his big discovery day, Matthew had been hiking around with his father, Lee, a paleoanthropologist exploring outside Johannesburg, South Africa. The area where Matthew found the fossils is often called the Cradle of Humankind because so many old humanoid bones have been found there. Studying the bones Matthew found, scientists learned they came from a young boy about four feet (1.2 m) tall. With further digging in the area, Lee Berger found more of the young male's skull and other bones. Matthew continued to go out on fossil hunts with his dad and, in 2013, wriggled his way into a limestone cave where some amateur explorers had seen bones. Matthew took pictures of the fossils, and his father recruited people small enough to fit into the cave to retrieve the bones. They found more than 1,500.

PETRIFIED WOOD & AMBER

• LIFE GETS HARD •

PETRIFIED WOOD, ARIZONA, U.S.A.

Get me outta here!

I thought we were pals!

Not all fossils end up trapped in stone. *Wood* you believe some ancient trees actually turn into stone? And there's nothing sappy about this: Resin, a sap-like substance in some ancient trees, sometimes hardened around living creatures. The hardened goo became what's called amber, and some creatures became trapped inside.

TREE-MENDOUS FOSSILS

Water, ash, and minerals have all played a part in turning trees into fossils. Hundreds of millions of years ago, mud and water that left sediment on fallen trees

So close, yet so far!

ONE **100-MILLION-YEAR-OLD** PIECE OF **AMBER** HELD A **SPIDER** ATTACKING A **WASP** CAUGHT IN THE **SPIDER'S WEB.**

and branches slowed the process of decay that would normally rot a dead tree. In some areas, volcanic ash also covered the downed trees. Over time, minerals in the ash and sediment replaced the trees' organic matter. The minerals turned the trees into rocks and often left colorful patterns inside them as well.

FROM GOO TO GEM

Conifer trees, the ones with cones, ooze out resin to protect themselves when they're damaged. But not all hardened tree resin is amber. It usually takes 100,000 years or more for the liquid to harden enough to make the grade. The oldest known amber is 320 million years old.

Ancient Greeks thought amber held trapped sunlight, and while it can't trap those rays, it can trap air and water bubbles, as well as insects and other living things. Scientists have found complete insects inside amber, as well as animal bones and lizards. Inside one lizard stuck in amber was an ant it had eaten. Another piece of amber trapped a 100-million-year-old female insect carrying eggs. Amber that doesn't have creatures inside it is prized as a gem.

BALTIC BONANZA

For centuries, people have valued amber for its beautiful color. It has often been turned into gems, and in the 18th century, a Prussian ruler named Friedrich I used several tons of it to line the walls of a room in his palace. When the ruler of Russia, Tsar Peter I (also known today as Peter the Great) saw this amber room, he said how much he liked it. Friedrich's son, Frederick William I, who was now king, decided to give Peter the room. The Prussian ruler took the room apart and shipped it in 18 boxes to his friend.

Prussia is now part of Germany. Today, it and Russia are just two of the countries that border the Baltic Sea. The region around the sea produces what is considered the best amber for use as gems.

WHERE IN THE WORLD? A FOREST OF FOSSILS

To see one of the largest collections of petrified wood in the world, head to Petrified Forest National Park in Arizona, U.S.A. The stone fossils there are more than 200 million years old!

In ancient times, rivers flowed through what is now desert. The water carried dead trees along, and sometimes a group of trees formed a logjam, creating the small forests of petrified trees featured in the park today. Some of the trees look like they've been sawed into pieces, though they actually broke naturally. The quartz inside the rock trees makes them very brittle and easy to break. Millions of years ago, as the land in the region shifted, the trees broke apart.

MINERALS
• THE INSIDE STORY •

Mohs
definitely

BY THE NUMBERS

Geologists rate the hardness of rocks and minerals on a scale from 1 to 10. It's named for the man who created it, Friedrich Mohs.

MINERAL	HARDNESS
Talc	1
Gypsum	2
Calcite	3
Fluorite	4
Apatite	5
Orthoclase	6
Quartz	7
Topaz	8
Corundum	9
Diamond	10

When you look at a rock, you see a solid chunk of stuff. What you might not be able to see are the minerals that are inside almost all rocks. Minerals are everywhere—there are more than 5,000 different ones on Earth, and they exist on other planets, too. Not all of them are commonly found in rocks—fewer than a hundred make up most of Earth's crust. Of these, a handful of minerals, like feldspar, mica, and quartz, are extremely common "ingredients" in rocks. They're sort of like salt, sugar, and flour to a baker—you couldn't make much without them.

What makes one mineral different from another? The key lies in things you cannot even see, even with a powerful microscope. All substances are made up of tiny particles called atoms. Each mineral's atoms come together to form crystals in a particular way. This crystal structure is one way geologists tell minerals apart.

IT'S ELEMENTAL

Most minerals are made up of two or more elements—these are substances that can't be broken down into simpler substances with the same chemical properties. They're the basic building blocks of all the gas, liquids, and solids in the world, and some help keep you alive, like oxygen. It's part of the air you breathe and the water you drink. And it turns up in lots of rocks, too, because lots of minerals have oxygen in them. Oxygen is one of the 118 chemical elements known to exist.

A PROPER LOOK AT MINERAL PROPERTIES

A property might be a nice piece of land, so minerals must be pretty rich since they have lots of properties! Not exactly. Properties are what geologists call the various traits or features that make one mineral different from another. Crystal form is one property. Some of the others are how hard the mineral is and its luster, which describes how light reflects off a mineral. (Some shine in the light, while others are dull.) Another mineral property is its streak—the color it leaves when it's rubbed on a white porcelain tile.

RARE FARE

Want to see the mineral fingerite disappear? You don't need to find a magician—just expose it to water. Fingerite is one of the world's rarest minerals. It's found in only one spot on Earth—near the top of Izalco volcano in El Salvador. Fingerite can exist for years if the weather stays dry. But when it starts to rain, the mineral just washes away.

The kiwi to grape health

DID YOU KNOW?
FOOD FOR THOUGHT

Minerals aren't just found in rocks. They're inside you, and they keep your body running like a well-oiled machine. Plants absorb minerals from the soil, and animals get minerals from the plants they eat. When we eat these plants or animals, we get minerals from them. We can also get minerals by taking pills packed with them. The most important elements that come from minerals and keep us healthy include calcium, potassium, and sodium. They turn up in rocks, too, but don't try to eat one to get your daily dose of minerals!

MINERALS
• MORE ABOUT MINERALS •

BAUXITE

PAY DIRT!

At the New Mexico Mineral Museum in Socorro, New Mexico, U.S.A., minerals are the star of the show. On display are more than 5,000 different minerals.

Some of the minerals found in rocks are the source of metals we use every day. That piece of aluminum foil wrapped around leftovers in the fridge? It probably started out as a piece of bauxite that might have come from a mine in Australia. And some of the most valuable materials on Earth, such as gold and platinum, are also classified as minerals.

Minerals are the source of most of the world's gemstones, as well. Rough pieces of a mineral are cut and polished, so they can be worn as beautiful jewelry. As you'll learn later, the rarest and most valuable gemstones are called precious gems. Diamonds fall into that category. Others are less valuable or rare—though people still like and wear them. These are called semiprecious gems.

• KEEPING IT CLASSY •

You probably share some traits with other students in your classes, like your age and where you live. Well, minerals are like that, too. Depending on the elements inside of them, minerals are grouped into different classes. The biggest mineral clan is the silicates—minerals made up primarily of oxygen and silicon, with some other elements mixed in. Here's a quick look at the other major mineral classes.

BORATE: formed when oxygen combines with a form of the element boron

CARBONATES: minerals with carbon and oxygen, along with an element, such as calcium

HALIDES: any of several elements, such as chlorine or fluorine, combined with a metal

HYDROXIDES: formed when water combines with a metallic element

OXIDES: formed when oxygen combines with a metal, such as iron

NATIVE ELEMENTS: minerals that have only one element, such as gold and silver

SULFATES: chemical compounds composed of one sulfur atom with four oxygen atoms surrounding it

SULFIDES: formed when sulphur combines with a metal, such as lead

GOLD

• USEFUL AND RARE •

I am truly stunning

FAST STATS

HARDNESS:
2.5-3

STREAK:
Golden yellow

LUSTER:
Metallic

The gold standard, the golden rule, a heart of gold, the golden age—these expressions and many more show how fascinated people are with this precious metal. And why not? Gold is rare, it's beautiful, and it has plenty of uses. You can find it in jewelry, coins, spacecraft—even in food! And because gold doesn't corrode, it keeps its beautiful shine for thousands of years.

Crikey!

WHAT'S THOUGHT TO BE THE **LARGEST GOLD NUGGET** EVER FOUND WAS UNCOVERED NEAR KAMBALDA, IN WESTERN **AUSTRALIA,** IN 2018. IT **WEIGHED 198 POUNDS** (90 KG).

A GOLD MINE OF FACTS

Gold is a native element. It's found in all three types of rocks, forming streaks called veins. A deposit of gold in a rock is called a lode. When someone says they've hit the mother lode, they mean that they've found a lot of something valuable, even if it's not gold.

Miners look for gold in rocks, but they also find gold at the bottom of rivers and streams. That's because flecks of the metal break off from the lodes through weathering and end up in the water. Scientists estimate that, so far, people have recovered around 200,000 tons (181,437 t) of gold from the planet.

The quality of gold is measured in karats (not carats, which you'll read about later, or carrots, which you should eat). This measurement shows how much gold is in an alloy, or mixture of metals. Based on a total of 24 parts, a 14-karat ring has 14 parts of gold and 10 parts of another metal. So, 24-karat gold is pure gold. And gold is so special that it has its own system for weight. An ounce of gold is called a troy ounce (31 g) and weighs a bit more than a regular ounce. The value of an ounce of gold changes over time. In 2011, the price briefly soared to more than $1,900 per ounce, a record for the time.

But all that glitters is not gold, as the saying goes. A mineral called pyrite is often confused for gold, since it's a similar color and has the same luster. This gold impostor is often called fool's gold. But finding it can be helpful for a gold prospector, as the fake gold and the real thing are sometimes found near each other.

RUSHING FOR RICHES

People have mined gold for more than 5,000 years, but one discovery of the yellow mineral was a true golden moment. In 1848, James Marshall was building a sawmill along the American River in California, U.S.A., not far from an area called Coloma. Marshall looked in the water at the mill, and a sparkle caught his eye. He had spotted flecks of gold! Unsurprisingly, he and his partner, John Sutter, tried to keep the discovery secret. But the news that gold could be found near what is now known as Sutter's Mill soon spread. The great California gold rush was underway. Over the next few years, miners found about $2 billion worth of gold. About 90 percent of all the gold ever mined anywhere in the world was mined after 1848.

PYRITE, ALSO KNOWN AS FOOL'S GOLD

GOING FOR THE GOLD

• IT REALLY PANS OUT •

What's gold got that makes people crave it? Well, it's rare and it's beautiful. But the metal also comes in handy, and not just as rings. Gold is easy to shape into jewelry, but it can also be pounded into thin sheets or wires. An ounce of gold could be turned into a single wire (thinner than a human hair!) about 50 miles (80 km) long. Here are just some of the ways people have used gold throughout history.

GOLD JEWELRY

To show off their wealth, the world's richest people have often worn gold jewelry. Sometimes they've also worn clothes with gold threads in them. Even the rough-and-tumble Vikings of Scandinavia liked to show off with gold duds! One of the greatest pieces of gold jewelry known was made for King Tutankhamun. The Egyptians made a mask of gold with his facial features and then placed it in the tomb with his mummy. The mask was made out of 22.5 pounds (10.2 kg) of gold.

GOLD MONEY

Gold was one of the earliest forms of money. When ancient people wanted to buy something, they might have used gold nuggets or coins made from the mineral. More than 2,000 years ago in Rome, the great general Julius Caesar rewarded his soldiers with pieces of gold.

Pass me a slice

IN 2007, THE CANADIAN GOVERNMENT MADE A **$1 MILLION GOLD COIN.** IT WEIGHED **220 POUNDS** (100 KG) AND WAS AS BIG AS A **LARGE PIZZA!**

GOLD IN MEDICINE

What's up, doc? For a long time, the answer has often been gold. Doctors and dentists have used gold and gold alloys in many ways. Some ancient people replaced lost teeth with animal teeth held together with thin strips of gold. Later, gold was used to replace entire teeth. In the early part of the 21st century, dentists around the world were filling their patients' mouths with 77 tons (70 t) of gold each year! And gold can even be used to (help) cure what ails you—if you have the eye condition known as lagophthalmos, that is. With that condition, patients can't close their eyes all the way. Doctors sometimes insert tiny gold weights into their upper lids so they'll close again.

Far out

GOLD IN SPACE

Gold comes from the ground, but you can find it in outer space, too. That's because it reflects light and other forms of energy. For astronauts, a thin layer of gold on their helmet visors helps shield them from heat and radiation. These same thin sheets of gold protect satellites, too. And like computers and other devices on Earth, satellites rely on gold to conduct electrical signals.

I'm fillin' good

GOLD IN FOOD

If you are what you eat, then some people are really golden! For centuries, some chefs have added tiny bits of gold to their fanciest dishes—from sushi to doughnuts to chicken wings. To be safe, edible gold has to be at least 23 karat. If it's less pure than that, the other metals in it could make you sick.

GOLD IN ELECTRONICS

All aboard! Gold is a great conductor—wait, not that kind of conductor. Gold is good for conducting, or carrying, electronic signals. Because of that, small amounts of it are used in computer memory chips and other electronic devices. And since gold doesn't corrode, it lasts a long time in these devices. Your smartphone has a tiny amount of gold in it, too, but don't try to mine it: It's not worth that much, and you'd just break your phone. Of course, if you need a new phone and really like gold, you can get one from the British company Stuart Hughes that is made almost entirely of the shiny metal for just $15 million!

SILVER
• SECOND TO NONE •

WHAT'S IN A NAME?

All native elements have a chemical symbol, and silver's is Ag. That comes from the Latin word *argentum*, which describes how silver looks: white and shining.

Silver medals go to second-place winners in sporting events, but there's nothing second-rate about this native element. It has almost as many uses as gold; unlike that precious metal, however, silver will tarnish, or turn dark, when exposed to air. But a little polish and some elbow grease can bring back silver's shine.

IN INDIA, SILVER IS SOMETIMES TURNED INTO **THIN SHEETS** CALLED **CHANDI-KA-WARQ,** OR *VARAK*, THAT ARE USED TO **DECORATE** DESSERTS.

A PIECE OF SILVER HISTORY

Arrrgh, matey! Some pirate lore has helped keep the name of an old silver coin alive. The 1883 book *Treasure Island* by Robert Louis Stevenson features pirates—one of them, incidentally, called Long John Silver—who refer to "pieces of eight," an English name for a Spanish silver coin called an "eight-reales." The reale was a unit of currency in Spain, so one piece of eight was worth eight reales. Starting in the 1500s, Spain mined huge amounts of silver in its colonies of Mexico, Bolivia, and Peru, and some of the metal was turned into reales. These were used wherever the Spanish traded, and for a time, they were common in North America, too. If people needed to make change, they cut a coin into smaller pieces. One-fourth of a piece of eight was equal to two reales and was called two bits.

A STERLING MINERAL AND METAL

Silver is not as rare as gold, so it's not as valuable. But like gold, it has been used as money and jewelry for ages. Silver mining began in what is now Anatolia, Turkey, more than 5,000 years ago. Silver is a native element, though it's often found mixed with other minerals or metals such as zinc and lead. It's commonly uncovered in igneous rocks.

As a metal, silver by itself is too soft to be made into jewelry and other items, so small amounts of other metals are added to it. Usually the second metal is copper, and the alloy made is called sterling silver. Sterling is 92.5 percent silver.

DID YOU KNOW?
SAYING A MOUTHFUL

Like gold, silver has worked its way into common English phrases. Someone said to be born with a silver spoon in their mouth comes from a wealthy family. And if that mouth has a silver tongue, it means the person is one smooth talker. In myths, firing a silver bullet is one way to kill a werewolf; a silver bullet is a term that means something that can easily solve a tough problem. And when you try to find something good in a mostly rotten situation, you're looking for a silver lining.

Keep that silver away!

SILVER

• HERE, THERE & EVERYWHERE •

ure, you can see silver items in jewelry stores or on display in museums. But like gold, this precious metal turns up in lots of places you might not expect. Here are some more of the surprising ways we use silver.

① MIRRORS

Mirror, mirror, on the wall, what reflects best of all? It's silver! Silver reflects light better than any other metal, so it's used to make many mirrors. A piece of glass goes over the silver, which is often coated with copper or other materials on its back side. Silver's ability to reflect so well also makes it useful in some windows. The glass is coated with a layer of silver that lets in some light while reflecting back some of the sun's heat. That helps keep modern skyscrapers with lots of windows stay cool.

Bad news travels fast

② PAUL REVERE

One of history's most famous silversmiths was Paul Revere. There was no horsing around in his Boston shop—though Revere did take time in April 1775 to take part in a famous ride, helping to warn American colonists that the British were on the march. The next day, the American Revolution began. Some silver items that Revere made are now worth tens of thousands of dollars.

③ PHOTOGRAPHS

Actors dream of making it big on the silver screen—ever wonder where that expression came from? Well, back in the day, movie screens had some silver in them. The silver reflected light, so the image on the screen was easier to see. Silver was also a key part of some of the first photographs, which appeared during the 1830s. A silver compound was put onto a copper plate, slid into a camera, and then exposed to light, which created an image on the plate. Glass plates later replaced the copper ones, but silver was still part of the process for capturing an image. When film for cameras was developed, silver was part of the film, too, and medical x-ray film still contains silver. Even photographers who shoot with digital cameras rely on silver. When they print out their pictures, the paper often contains tiny bits of the metal.

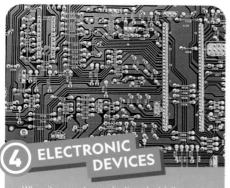

④ ELECTRONIC DEVICES

When it comes to conducting electricity, no metal does it better than silver. In fact, all other metals' ability to carry an electrical jolt is compared to silver's conductivity. And silver is tops when it comes to conducting heat, too. Being such a good conductor makes silver a key part of many electronic devices. The circuit boards inside computers contain silver, and if you recycled one million typical smartphones, you'd find 772 pounds (350 kg) of silver. A form of silver made into a paste is also used in solar panels, which turn sunlight into electricity.

⑤ CUTLERY

Skilled craftspeople, called silversmiths, have been turning silver into useful objects for a long time. Silver knives and forks were some of these everyday items, but silver was too expensive for most people to afford. Silver-plated "silverware" came along in the 1740s, when an English silver company found a way to put a layer of silver over copper (a process called plating). That made silverware more affordable. Today, though, most silverware is actually made from stainless steel.

Smell ya later

⑥ OINTMENTS

When it comes to battling bacteria, doctors may have a silver bullet with real silver. People have known for centuries that silver can kill the microscopic critters that cause many illnesses and infections. In the past, doctors wrapped wounds with thin pieces of silver to keep the bacteria out. Some patients even swallowed a form of silver to fight illnesses. (Never *ever* do this.) Today, some creamy medicines with silver, called ointments, are spread on burns and wounds to prevent infection. And some clothes have tiny pieces of silver in them to help kill the bacteria that cause body odor!

LOST AT SEA
• BURIED AND SUNKEN TREASURE •

Finders, keepers! Whether it's gold jewelry, silver pieces of eight, or precious gems, people love the idea of hunting—and finding!—lost treasure. Some has been buried on land; some was lost at sea. But wherever it turns up, treasure reveals bits of history ... and sometimes makes the treasure seekers very rich!

ARCTIC OCEAN

NORTH AMERICA

ATLANTIC OCEAN

PACIFIC OCEAN

SOUTH AMERICA

OFF THE COAST OF SOUTH CAROLINA

The United States stretches from "sea to shining sea," and for a time, some of that shine may have come from sunken gold. During the 1850s, when miners struck gold in California, some of it was shipped as bars and coins. The best way to transport the wealth was on ships that sailed around South America to the eastern United States., like the S.S. *Central America*. In 1857, stormy weather swamped the ship on one of its voyages, sending tons of gold, along with silver and jewelry, into the ocean depths. The wreckage site was found in 1987, and since then, gold worth more than $50 million has been recovered.

OFF THE COAST OF CARTAGENA, COLOMBIA

Sailors on the Spanish ship *San José* got a sinking feeling in 1708. They had lost a sea battle with a British ship and sunk—along with the cargo of gold, silver, and gems they were bringing back to Spain. The remains of the ship were found in 2015. The Colombian government hopes to soon begin searching for the precious cargo that went down with the *San José*, which would today be worth billions of dollars.

CUERDALE, ENGLAND

The Vikings of Scandinavia once roamed over large parts of Europe, including England. In 1840, some men working along a river near Preston, Lancashire, found a collection of their silver coins and jewelry known today as the Cuerdale Hoard. Buried in a chest were more than 8,000 items dating back almost 1,000 years.

HOXNE VILLAGE, ENGLAND

Sometimes, you don't need fancy equipment to find buried treasure. Eric Lawes hit the nail on the head when he went searching for a lost hammer with a simple metal detector. The detector went crazy, and Lawes started digging, helping to uncover what's now called the Hoxne Hoard. The treasure dates to the fifth century A.D. and includes more than 15,000 Roman coins, silver spoons, and 200 gold objects. Altogether, the silver and gold weighed about 60 pounds (27 kg). Lawes and the farmer who owns the land where he found the hoard split about $2 million. And Lawes also found his lost hammer.

EUROPE

ASIA

AFRICA

INDIAN OCEAN

AUSTRALIA

THE MOUTH OF THE NILE RIVER, EGYPT

Some people find treasure on the ocean's bottom; not many uncover a sunken city. But that's just what archaeologist Franck Goddio did in 2000, when he found the remains of a city called Heracleion. Once a bustling seaport used by the ancient Greeks, the city was hit by earthquakes and other natural disasters that buried it under sand some 1,200 years ago. Goddio thinks he and his team have found only a small part of the port. So far, they have uncovered bronze statues, coins, jewelry, and a piece of a giant granite statue of an ancient god.

TILLYA TEPE, AFGHANISTAN

In ancient times, Afghanistan was part of a trade route that stretched between Asia and Europe. You could call it the country's golden age, and the items found at Tillya Tepe prove it. The name of the site means "the hill of gold," and in 1978, some 20,000 gold items were discovered there in six burial mounds. The items are about 2,000 years old and include a gold crown, a silver mirror from China, and a gold coin from the Roman Empire.

DIAMONDS
• TOUGH STUFF •

When you want to talk tough, talk diamond. This mineral is the hardest substance known, and nothing can scratch its surface—except another diamond! Diamonds are made from atoms of the element carbon that are grouped tightly together, which is why they're so tough.

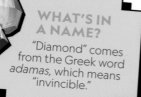

WHAT'S IN A NAME?

"Diamond" comes from the Greek word *adamas*, which means "invincible."

GOING UP

Diamonds form under intense heat and pressure in the mantle, the layer of Earth just below the crust. This process has been going on for a long time: Some diamonds formed 4.3 billion years ago! They made

Whoa, Nelly!

THE REMAINS OF A DISTANT **BURNED-OUT WHITE DWARF STAR** ARE MADE OF **HARDENED CARBON,** MAKING IT A **GIANT DIAMOND.**

their way upward when volcanic eruptions brought up rocks in the mantle that had diamonds in them. Miners today dig through these diamond-toting rocks. Many diamonds are found in the rock kimberlite, but people sometimes also find diamonds on the ground, after the rock that carried them to the surface has eroded away.

GOOD JUNK

Because diamonds are rare and have a beautiful sparkle, they are often turned into gemstones and used in jewelry (see page 156). But diamonds have a practical use, too. While most don't have the looks to be gemstones, they sparkle in another way. These "junk" diamonds, also called bort, are incredibly useful in industry. Tiny bits of diamond on drills and saws turn them into super cutters, able to slice through rocks and even other diamonds. Diamonds are also used to grind down other materials, and diamond "dust" often ends up in a paste jewelers and others use as a polish.

BY THE NUMBERS

On Earth's surface, diamonds are rare. But go down around **100 MILES** (161 km) below the surface and it's a different story. Some scientists have estimated there may be **MORE THAN A QUADRILLION TONS** (.91 quadrillion t)—that's a one followed by 15 zeros!—of diamonds locked in rocks in Earth's interior.

WHERE IN THE WORLD?
ONE BIG PIT

If you dig holes, you'd love the Mirny Mine. Located in eastern Siberia, Russia, the mine is one of the largest holes ever dug by humans. It's 1,722 feet (525 m) deep and 3,900 feet (1,189 m) wide—that's more than half a mile! The pit contained kimberlite filled with diamonds, and for a time, miners there were hauling out 4,400 pounds (2,000 kg) of diamonds each year. The open-pit mine closed in 2001, but a Russian diamond company still mines underground in Mirny.

Some people claim that the giant hole can cause helicopters flying over it to lose control and crash. The theory says that warm air collects in the pit and then rises above it, while cold air from outside rushes in to take its place. The quick change in temperature and the difference in airflow causes a spinning vortex that could send a chopper crashing. But that's just a theory—no one has ever seen a helicopter go down over the pit. In 2010, a Russian company had an idea for putting the hole to good use: It wanted to build a domed city in it. But unlike helicopters, the idea never got off the ground.

METEORITES
• MINERALS FROM THE SKIES •

Look out belooow!

A MAN IN MICHIGAN, U.S.A., **USED A ROCK** AS A DOORSTOP, UNTIL HE FOUND OUT IT **WAS A METEORITE WORTH $100,000!**

Not all diamonds come from deep within Earth. A small number hitch a ride here on meteorites—the remains of extraterrestrial impactors found on Earth. Some space diamonds discovered in 2015 probably formed inside what scientists call protoplanets. These large bodies of matter were created in our solar system before Earth but then broke apart. Protoplanets could have had enough heat and pressure inside them to create diamonds, just as they form here on Earth.

CLASS ACTS

Diamonds aren't the only minerals that rocket their way to Earth inside meteorites. Many of those space stones contain iron.

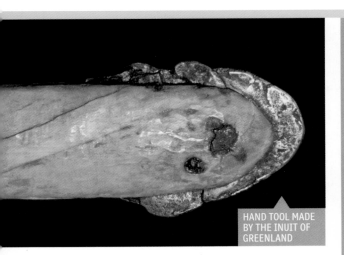

HAND TOOL MADE BY THE INUIT OF GREENLAND

MAKING AN IMPACT

Most meteorites that reach Earth are pretty puny—barely bigger than a piece of dust. But every once in a while, a real whopper strikes the planet, leaving a huge dent called an impact crater. Geologists have found more than 100 impact craters on Earth. The largest single crater is thought to be one in South Africa, called Vredefort crater, formed about two billion years ago and estimated to have been about 186 miles (300 km) wide when it was first created. Erosion at the site, however, has made it hard for scientists to get an exact figure.

So, what's the largest meteorite ever found on Earth? A 66-ton (60-t) mass of metal discovered on a farm called Hoba West in the African nation of Namibia in 1920. The iron meteorite is now a tourist attraction and a Namibian national monument.

Scientists group meteorites into three major classes: iron, stone, and stony-iron. Iron meteorites are almost all iron (with some nickel) and are heavy compared with a rock of a similar size. Stone meteorites look like stones you might find on Earth, but some are more attractive—to magnets, that is: The iron and nickel inside make them magnetic, just as iron meteorites are. In the stony-iron class, a meteorite has about an equal mix of rock and metal. These are the least common of the three main classes of meteorites found on Earth.

For ancient peoples, iron found in meteorites could make their lives easier. In Egypt, they mined the mineral and made what they called "metal from heaven." As many as 5,000 years ago, they used iron to make beads and other items, including, most likely, the blade of a knife found in King Tutankhamun's tomb. In Greenland, a people known today as the Inuit used space iron to craft knives and other weapons.

ROCK STAR

SOLVING A DEADLY MYSTERY

What wiped out the dinosaurs around 66 million years ago? Walter Alvarez found a clue in 1977. The geologist discovered a 66-million-year-old clay layer that contained a lot of the element iridium, which often turns up in meteorites. Alvarez thought that a huge asteroid colliding with Earth around that time could have created a cloud all over the world and reduced how much sunlight reached the ground, killing the dinosaurs and a lot of other animals alive at the time. There was only one problem with Alvarez's theory—no one could prove that an asteroid large enough to affect life on Earth had struck the planet back then. But then, during the 1990s, scientists found the smoking gun—or hole: a huge impact crater buried under Mexico's Yucatán Peninsula that was 66 million years old. The asteroid that made it barreled into Earth at 40,000 miles an hour (64,374 km/h) and left a crater 115 miles (185 km) wide. The scientific world now accepts Alvarez's idea about the connection between the asteroid collision and the end of the age of the dinosaurs.

PLATINUM
• ALMOST AS GOOD AS GOLD •

FAST STATS

HARDNESS:
4–4.5

STREAK:
Silvery gray or other shades of gray

LUSTER:
Metallic

WHAT'S IN A NAME?

"Platinum" comes from the Spanish word *platina*, which means "little silver."

To the Spanish who came to South America looking for gold and silver, platinum was a puzzle. It looked like silver, and it turned up with both silver and gold in rocks, but the Spaniards couldn't melt it like silver. To them, the mineral was worthless, and they'd toss it aside. Today, we know how wrong they were!

Platinum is another rare and valuable native element—it's actually rarer than gold. And it's hard to produce. Miners need to dig up several tons of rocks to produce one troy ounce (31 g) of pure platinum. Platinum rarely turns up in large nuggets as gold sometimes does. Instead, it's usually found in pockets called placer deposits at the bottom of streams.

I'm kind of a big deal

PLATINUM'S PALS

Sometimes platinum is also found in rocks with one or more related silvery metals. Together, they are known as the platinum group. The other members of this band are iridium, osmium, palladium, rhodium, and ruthenium. Um, that's a lot of "ums"! All six metals are good catalysts, which means they can speed up how other chemicals react with each other, without changing themselves.

PAY DIRT!

Musicians who sell one million copies of a recording get what's called a platinum album, but the award is really just platinum-colored plastic.

BEST ROCK BAND

DID YOU KNOW?
A WHEELY USEFUL MINERAL

When you're out driving around in a car or van, platinum is there with you. Those spark plugs that get a gas engine going have tips coated with platinum, since the metal stays hard even at temperatures up to about 3200°F (1760°C). And platinum, along with its metallic buddy palladium, helps take pollution out of a car's exhaust. They're also used in parts called catalytic converters, which turn the harmful chemicals produced when gas is burned into safer chemicals. Around the world, about half of the platinum mined each year goes into cars and other vehicles. But that could change in years to come. More electric cars should be hitting the road, and—because they don't burn gas—they don't use spark plugs or catalytic converters.

COPPER
• ANOTHER ELEMENTAL METAL •

FAST STATS

HARDNESS:
2.5–3
STREAK:
Metallic
copper red
LUSTER:
Metallic

BY THE NUMBERS

In cars, copper goes into wires and other parts. The average small car has about **44 POUNDS** (20 kg) **OF COPPER** in it.

Vroom, vroom

It's easy to cop an attitude about copper. This native element is one source for another amazingly useful metal.

Pure nuggets of copper sometimes appear in streams or buried in the ground. Most copper is found in igneous rocks, though sedimentary rocks sometimes have it as well. Copper usually occurs in an ore, combined with other minerals. Chalcopyrite, a mixture of copper, iron, and a form of sulfur, is mined to produce much of the world's copper.

COPPING SOME COPPER HISTORY

When early humans began replacing their stone tools with ones made of metal, they turned to copper. They began working with the metal about 10,000 years ago, taking the pure nuggets they found and hammering them into sheets. Next, these sheets were shaped into objects, such as weapons, axes, and jewelry. A few thousand years later, metalsmiths began using heat to remove copper trapped inside ores, providing a greater supply of the metal. Why was copper a cut above the old stone weapons and cutting tools? It was lighter, more flexible, and easier to sharpen than stone.

In North America, Native Americans made copper objects starting at least 6,000 years ago. Much of the copper came from areas around what is today Wisconsin and Michigan, and they traded some of it as far away as what is now Georgia. Much, much later, when U.S. settlers spread across the country, they found copious copper deposits in Michigan's Upper Peninsula. Between 1845 and 1968, miners dug out more than 5.5 million tons (5 million t) of copper in one part of the region. In 1997, after the mines had closed, two men using a metal detector found a single piece of copper that weighed 26.6 tons (24.1 t), making it the largest copper "nugget" ever.

COPPER ALL AROUND

People don't swing copper axes anymore, but the mineral turns up all around us. Chances are, when you throw a light switch, the electricity is flowing through copper wires since copper is a great conductor of electricity. The plumbing in your house might have copper pipes, too. And because it conducts heat well, copper also turns up in cookware.

That's a big welcome

THE COPPER LADY

Looking out over the harbor in New York City is one giant lady: the Statue of Liberty. Completed in 1886 with an estimated 200,000 pounds (90,720 kg) of copper, "Lady Liberty" was a gift to the United States from France. From the base of the pedestal foundation to the tip of her torch, the statue is 305.5 feet (93 m) tall—the tallest copper statue in the United States. Originally, Lady Liberty was a reddish color, like copper itself, but over time she's turned a shade of green. That's a natural process that occurs when copper is exposed to the oxygen in air.

A FORM OF COPPER **IN THE** BLOOD OF **SOME OCTOPUSES** HELPS CARRY **OXYGEN** THROUGH THEIR BODY—AND **MAKES** THEIR BLOOD BLUE!

DID YOU KNOW? COPPER CURES

Some doorknobs are made from a copper alloy. Like silver, copper is a bacteria killer, so using copper alloys in public places can stop the spread of disease. Some hospitals have drastically limited infections by using copper alloys on surfaces patients touch often. And using copper in medicine is not new: Ancient doctors used copper to treat wounds or as part of medicines, and some people used it to purify drinking water.

THE BRONZE AGE
• AN EXCELLENT ALLOY •

You're a real
status cymbal

MAP OF THE STARS

A disc found on the ground may show how some ancient people saw the sky. In 1999, treasure hunters using a metal detector found a round piece of bronze near Nebra, Germany. Known as the Nebra Sky Disc, it's about 12 inches (30.5 cm) in diameter and decorated with gold shapes that seem to represent the stars, the moon, and the sun. Why was the more than 3,000-year-old disc made? Some people think it may have been a crude map of the universe as seen by the Bronze Age citizens of Nebra. The ancient farmers might have used it to determine the best time to plant their crops, based on the sun's position during the longest and shortest days of the year.

It takes two to tango—or to make a great alloy, at least. Some of copper's alloys have proved to be marvelous metals, too. The first of these alloys to make an impact on history was bronze. Starting almost 6,000 years ago, metalsmiths in the Middle East mixed a lot of copper with a bit of tin, and *voilà*—they had a new metal. And a medal-winning metal it was: Bronze was harder than copper alone, and it was easier to melt and then pour into molds to make metal casts. The metalworkers used the casts to make such things as spear heads and wine cups. Other metals might also be mixed in, but copper and tin are still the main ingredients in bronze.

A METAL FOR THE AGES

The use of bronze appeared in different places at different times. But in any region, the time period when bronze became a common material is called the Bronze Age. In most of Europe, tin was pretty rare, so some bronze items were made only for the wealthiest people. But in Italy, a people called the Etruscans had access to tin through trade and made many daily items, such as dishes and utensils, out of bronze. And this is straight from the horse's mouth—the bits placed in horses' mouths were bronze, too. People in Europe also made armor out of bronze, and some of the great sculptures from ancient Greece and Rome were made of out of the metal.

Today, bronze might be best known in sports: The third-place finisher in an event often receives a bronze medal. (They're actually made out of brass, though, another copper alloy.) Some metal tools are made of bronze because they don't create sparks when they strike other metals. And bronze turns up in some musical instruments, too. That crash you hear when a drummer hits a cymbal? That usually comes from bronze. So does the strum that comes from many guitars, since their strings are often made of bronze.

INDIA'S STATUE OF UNITY—THE **TALLEST STATUE** IN THE WORLD AT **597 FEET** (182 M)—IS COVERED WITH **1,700 TONS** (1,542 T) **OF BRONZE.**

WHERE IN THE WORLD?
THE BRONZE VESSELS OF CHINA

Ships made of bronze? Not quite. These vessels were meant to hold liquids and foods during religious ceremonies. The first great makers of Chinese bronze worked near the Yellow River about 3,500 years ago. The vessels were made for China's rulers, who sometimes burned food in them as an offering to the dead. And when it came to making these bronze pieces, the artists really broke the mold.

Each piece was made with a mold that had inner and outer pieces of clay. (The inner piece showed the design of the finished vessel.) Molten bronze was poured between the two pieces of clay and allowed to cool. The artists then had to break the mold to remove the bronze, meaning no two vessels were exactly alike. Archaeologists first found the oldest of these bronze pieces in the city Anyang less than 100 years ago.

123

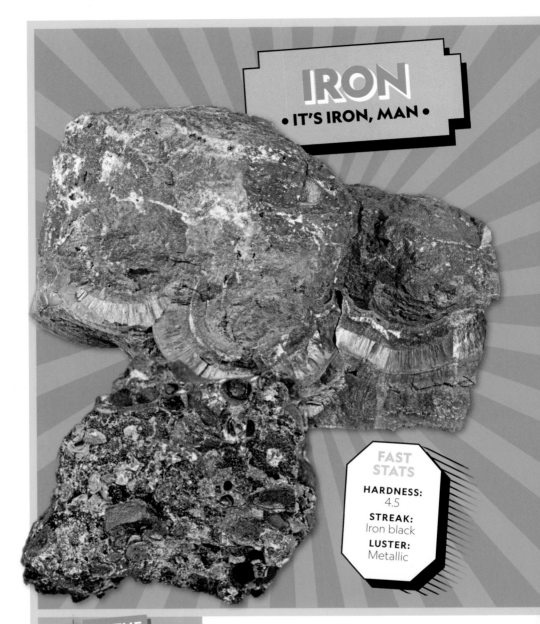

IRON
• IT'S IRON, MAN •

FAST STATS

HARDNESS:
4.5
STREAK:
Iron black
LUSTER:
Metallic

BY THE NUMBERS

The Eiffel Tower in Paris, France, is made of more than **18,000** pieces of wrought iron held together by **2.5 MILLION** rivets.

I f you could travel throughout the universe or into Earth's center, you'd find a whole lot of iron. It makes up most of Earth's core, as both a molten metal and a solid. And there's even iron in our bodies. It's part of something in our blood called hemoglobin, which not only makes blood red but also carries oxygen through our bodies.

Iron can be found as a native element, but it's usually mined as an ore in other minerals, such as hematite and magnetite. Much of the iron mined today is found in sedimentary rocks that began forming almost two billion years ago. Iron that was dissolved in seawater combined with oxygen to form common iron ores. The seawater eventually dried up, leaving the minerals behind.

PAY DIRT!

On Earth, hematite is the ore that provides the most iron. Hematite is also found on Mars and gives the planet its reddish glow, which is why it's often called the red planet. ("Hematite" comes from the Greek word for "blood.")

STEEL THE ONE

It's a good thing there's so much iron around because people have used it in so many ways. It's the main ingredient in steel, which turns up in buildings and vehicles of all kinds—from cars and trucks to ships and trains. You can find steel in your home, too, in major appliances and tiny paper clips. Steel is the world's most commonly used metal, and most of the iron mined around the world goes into making it.

Iron by itself also turns up in many things. Cooks like to use cast-iron pans because they're easy to clean and can go from the stovetop into an oven. Other items— such as fences and chairs—are made of wrought iron. That means a glob of hot iron is hammered and shaped as it cools. Blacksmiths once used wrought iron to make horseshoes, and some smiths still work iron this way.

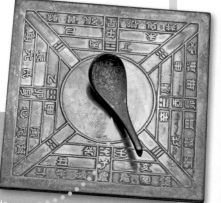

AN ATTRACTIVE ORE

Magnetite is a mixture of iron and oxygen that has quite a pull—a magnetic pull, that is. Thanks to the iron in it, magnetite is naturally magnetic. Lodestone is the name for magnetite used as a magnet, and about 2,400 years ago, the Chinese used lodestone as a pointer in compasses. The ore was carved into the shape of a spoon and then placed on a flat square of bronze. The end of the lodestone spoon always pointed south, attracted by the magnetic field that surrounds Earth.

Some of nature's critters have also found a use for magnetite. Tiny shellfish called chitons scrape their food off rocks using teeth on their tongues. What keeps the teeth strong and prevents them from breaking? It's not toothpaste—it's a layer of magnetite the chitons produce in their bodies that covers their teeth.

THE IRON AGE
• A CUT ABOVE •

Smelt ya later

Humans began using iron about 10,000 years ago, starting with iron that came to Earth in meteorites. But for centuries after, they continued to use copper and bronze for many tools and weapons. Then, about 3,000 years ago, people in parts of the Middle East and Europe realized iron was the better metal for everyday uses. It was much easier to find than the copper and tin needed to make bronze. That meant it was cheaper to make things out of iron. And iron actually created cutting tools with a sharper edge than ones made from stone. Plentiful and useful, iron made life easier for people around the world, and the Iron Age was born.

The Hittites, a people who lived in what is now Turkey, get the credit for perfecting iron smelting. Some of their most skilled blacksmiths could hammer and shape

BULGARIA

Black Sea

T U R K E Y

Mediterranean Sea

CYPRUS

SYRIA

LEBANON

IRAQ

Greatest extent of the Hittite Empire
Present-day countries are shown.

JORDAN

EGYPT

ISRAEL

wrought iron into pieces of art. As the knowledge of how to work with iron spread, it was used to make more things, such as cooking pots, nails, and tools of all kinds. Iron plows made farming easier, especially where the soil was thick with clay, as it was in England.

THE IRON AGE ARMIES

The Iron Age saw one great change from earlier periods. Rulers had amassed large armies before. But with iron, they could give their troops better weapons that were cheaper to make. Iron swords, knives, and spears became common on the battlefield. Commoners had to fight more often, as governments began to force them into military service. For officers, serving in the army could become a career, as rulers won new lands in battle and kept soldiers stationed in these foreign lands.

For archaeologists, weapons and other items from the Iron Age have revealed much about the era. In 2012, scientists working in Alken Enge, Denmark, found 2,000-year-old bones that indicated a large battle had been fought in the area. By 2018, the experts had collected more than 2,000 bones, some of which sported marks made by sharp weapons. The villages in the area were small, suggesting that someone had brought in soldiers from far and wide—several hundred were found at the battle site— to create this Iron Age army.

Ancient grave? On my way.

WHERE IN THE WORLD? THE EARLIEST IRONWORKS

While the Hittites are considered history's iron experts, Africa may lay claim to the oldest known site where iron was smelted. Slag is the waste product of iron smelting, and bits of slag about 4,000 years old have been found in Lejja, Nigeria. Some of the pieces of slag weigh as much as 132 pounds (60 kg).

DID YOU KNOW? BEATING THE BADGERS

In 2018, a U.S. military veteran was working with a team of archaeologists as part of Operation Nightingale, a program in which service members train with professional archaeologists. His group was trying to find burial sites at Barrow Clump, England, before the local badgers—yes, badgers!—did. These relatives of weasels love to dig—and their burrowing can disturb ancient graveyards before archaeologists have a chance to excavate them. Working with his metal detector, the veteran found the grave of a sixth-century Saxon warrior who had been buried with his sword, iron spear, and knife.

GRAPHITE
• ONE SLIPPERY MINERAL •

FAST STATS

HARDNESS:
1–2
STREAK:
Black
LUSTER:
Sub-metallic

A diamond is made up of carbon atoms, and so is graphite. But they're hardly carbon copies of each other. The arrangement of the carbon in graphite is much different—it forms a layer just one atom thick, and the chemical bonds between the atoms are weak. So, while a diamond is the hardest known substance, graphite is one of the softest.

A native element, graphite is found mostly in metamorphic rocks, such as gneiss, schist, and slate. Some turns up in basalt, too, and in iron meteorites. Graphite has a greasy feel, and that slippery quality makes it useful in industry. It's often used as a lubricant— a substance that makes solid objects slide easily against each other. Graphite is called a dry lubricant, unlike the wet oil that lubricates car parts and machinery. Some objects can be ruined if oil is used on them, so graphite is the slick choice instead.

HIGH HEAT? NO SWEAT!

Graphite is also able to withstand high temperatures—up to about 6500°F (3593°C). And as the temperature goes up past 1800°F (982°C), the material actually gets stronger. Since graphite stays solid when the heat is on, it's used in industries that use extreme temperatures to melt metal, such as the steel industry. And graphite's heat resistance makes it a preferred lubricant for car brakes. Brakes create a lot of heat when they slow wheels, and graphite makes sure they can keep doing their job.

Where else does graphite turn up? The mineral is used in nuclear reactors, which use the energy released by radioactive elements as they naturally break down. In this case, graphite is like a brake itself. It slows down the process that releases the energy, so engineers can control it. Graphite also conducts electricity well, so it's used in batteries like the ones that power smartphones and laptops. And for crooks, graphite can mean a ticket to jail: Police officers use a powder with graphite in it to look for fingerprints left at a crime scene.

THE MIRACLE MATERIAL

What bends like a piece of paper, conducts heat and electricity, and is stronger than steel or any other known material? Meet graphene, a wonder substance made from graphite. Scientists in Manchester, England, created it in the early 2000s by separating just a single layer of carbon atoms from a piece of graphite. A bit of graphite just .004 inch (.101 mm) thick has three million layers of graphene. And a string of graphene the width of a hair on your head is strong enough to lift a piano! Scientists think graphene can be used to make faster computers and improve medicines, along with many other uses.

GRAPHITE IS THE "LEAD" IN WOODEN PENCILS. IT'S SAID THAT THE **AVERAGE** WOODEN **PENCIL** HAS ENOUGH **GRAPHITE** TO DRAW A LINE **35 MILES** (56 KM) LONG.

MINERALS IN THE SEA
• WET RICHES AWAIT •

Look out below!

BY THE NUMBERS

It is estimated that about
20 MILLION POUNDS
(9.1 million kg) of gold is dissolved
in the world's waters. As of 2019,
that much gold would be worth
more than **$400 BILLION.**

There's gold in them thar waters—and lots of other minerals, too. The world's seas and oceans hold almost 50 different kinds of metals and minerals, and many of them are valuable. If you could extract all the minerals from these waters, they would weigh about 50 quadrillion tons (45.3 quadrillion t)!

But that's a big "if." Getting minerals out of water is more expensive than mining them on land. And the cost is even greater for minerals buried in the ocean floor or found along hydrothermal vents (see page 21).

THE DEAD SEA, A LAND-LOCKED SALT LAKE IN SOUTHWESTERN ASIA

At the bottom of the ocean, the water pressure that crushes against things is much greater than the pressure of air on land. Special, extra-strong equipment is needed to mine at depths of a mile or more.

THE MINERALS BELOW

Still, even with these challenges, some people think removing massive amounts of minerals from oceans and seas will one day be worth the cost. Besides gold, some of the minerals that interest mining companies include diamonds and ones that can be turned into metals, such as silver, copper, nickel, and aluminum. And some minerals can be taken from the ocean bottom, too.

Extracting minerals from the oceans and seas is not a new idea. For thousands of years, people have gotten sodium—salt—from seawater. Pools of water on land dried out, leaving salt behind. More recently, some of the world's magnesium has come from salty water, too. A form of the mineral called magnesium chloride is removed from water and heated. Then electricity separates the magnesium out of that compound. Magnesium is turned into a strong, lightweight metal that is usually part of an alloy, often with aluminum. When you drink something from a metal can, some of the magnesium in it might have come from the ocean or sea!

A GOLDEN DREAM

The idea came to Prescott Ford Jernegan in a dream—or so it was reported in 1897. Scientists had only recently discovered there was gold in seawater when Jernegan bragged that he could retrieve some of it, telling people he had invented a machine called a gold accumulator. Jernegan filled a box with chemicals and lowered it into the water off Connecticut, U.S.A. When he pulled out his device soon after, it was filled with gold! Investors gave Jernegan money so he could expand his gold mining efforts. But the investors soon learned that all that glitters is not gold. Jernegan had a partner who had secretly placed gold in the accumulator while it was in the water. The whole business was a scam! But it paid off for Jernegan and his partner, who made hundreds of thousands of dollars before fleeing the country.

WHERE IN THE WORLD?
MINING THE PACIFIC

The island nation of Papua New Guinea sits north of Australia—and near hydrothermal vents. In 2011, the country's government gave a Canadian company called Nautilus Minerals the right to remove minerals that collect near the vents. The deal is the first effort to mine the ocean deep for profit. The plan, according to Nautilus, is to knock down the "chimneys" of minerals that form as hot water from inside Earth meet the cold Pacific Ocean waters. Then, a giant hose will suck up the minerals, with the most valuable—gold and copper—removed from the mix. The company hopes to do similar mining off other Pacific islands. Some scientists, though, worry that the mining will kill rare life-forms found nowhere else on Earth. An organization called the International Seabed Authority is creating rules to lessen possible harmful impacts from deep-sea mining.

SILICATES

• NOTHING SILLY ABOUT SILICATES •

COLORFUL QUARTZ

FAST STATS: QUARTZ

HARDNESS:
7

STREAK:
White

LUSTER:
Vitreous (like glass)

on't look now, but we're surrounded by silicates. This group of minerals makes up 95 percent of Earth's crust and upper mantle. There are about 600 different kinds, and they all contain the elements silicon and oxygen, along with other elements. Silicates are found in all three types of rocks, and most of the minerals found in soils come from silicates.

A SINGLE QUARTZ CRYSTAL FOUND IN BRAZIL WEIGHED ALMOST 90,000 POUNDS (40,823 KG).

QWAZY ABOUT QUARTZ

When you stroll along some beaches, most of the sand you're walking on is often tiny bits of quartz. This silicate is one of the most common minerals on Earth's surface. It's also known as silica, and the presence of other chemical elements can give quartz different colors. Aluminum, for example, can make quartz dark, giving it the name smoky quartz. One form of quartz is called chalcedony. It's usually white, but it can take on other colors, too, when other elements get mixed in. The purest crystals of quartz are clear.

PUTTING QUARTZ TO GOOD USE

Sand that comes from quartz does a lot more than cover beaches and deserts. The purest silica sand, with almost no other minerals in it, is used to make glass. It's combined with other chemicals and then heated to more than 2450°F (1343°C)—hotter than molten lava! The liquid glass is then poured into molds so it can be turned into containers or other products. Quartz sand is also an ingredient in bricks and some concrete. The gritty feel of some sandpaper also comes from silica, and the sand that traps balls on a golf course is usually silica, too.

GLASSBLOWING

CHIP OFF THE OLD SILICA

What does sand have to do with your smartphone? The phone is like a mini computer and, like other computers, needs devices called chips to process information. These chips are made of silicon, and the source of most of this silicon is sand that came from quartz. The first silicon chip was invented in 1961. It was much smaller than earlier devices that sent electrical signals through computers. It was faster, too. Silicon was chosen because it was cheap and easier to work with than other materials. Today, the center of the high-tech industry in California, U.S.A., is called Silicon Valley.

MOON MESSAGES

In 1969, U.S. astronauts Neil Armstrong and Buzz Aldrin became the first humans to walk on the moon. They left behind a small silicon disc about the size of a half-dollar coin. On it, the United States had etched messages from several U.S. presidents and the leaders of 73 countries, in honor of the first moon landing. Each message was about the size of a pinhead and could be read only through a microscope. The scientists who developed the disc chose silicon because it was strong enough to withstand the extreme hot and cold temperatures found on the moon.

CLAYS
• CLAY ON DISPLAY •

With a little water and some heat, just about anybody can be an artist—as long as they also have some clay. People started making objects out of clay about 20,000 years ago, and they kept finding new uses for the different minerals that produce it.

Silicates are the main ingredient in most clays. The clay minerals often form from the weathering of such silicate minerals as feldspar and mica found in sedimentary and metamorphic rocks. A clay mineral called bentonite is usually found in volcanic rocks.

Clays absorb water easily, forming what looks like thick mud that can be shaped into pottery, from dishes to works of art. Then, at high heat, the clay becomes rock hard, and a piece of pottery can last for thousands of years—as long as no one drops it on the floor. Heated slabs of clay are also used as bricks and tiles in building construction.

KEY CLAYS

Two common clay minerals are kaolinite and bentonite. Kaolinite is the source of kaolin, which is used to make china—the fancy dishes many people use for special meals. Kaolin is also part of the mixture used to make porcelain, a fine ceramic material often used in art. Kaolin, though, doesn't just show up in dining rooms and museums. You could have some in your hands right now! Kaolin is often used to coat all kinds of paper, making it smooth and easy to print on. It also turns up in paint because it helps make the paint easier to apply.

Bentonite has many uses, too. It can help clarify liquids, such as honey and cooking oils, taking out gunk you don't want to eat. It also is added to laundry soap to help soften clothes. And if you have cats, they might be very familiar with bentonite: It helps form the scoopable clumps of litter in a litter box.

WHAT'S IN A NAME?

"Kaolin" comes from the Chinese word *Kao-ling*, now spelled *Gaoling*, meaning "high ridge."

Now that's a solid contribution

WHERE IN THE WORLD?
THE EMPEROR'S ETERNAL ARMY

An ancient Chinese army had feet of clay—and arms, torsos, and heads, too. In 1974, workers digging a well near Xi'an, China, discovered this group of life-size soldiers—thousands of them, along with clay horses pulling chariots. They were buried near the tomb of Qin Shi Huangdi, the first emperor of China, who ruled more than 2,200 years ago. Now called the terra-cotta warriors (terra-cotta refers to clay after it has been fired, or heated), the soldiers reflect the great skill of the artists who made them: Each of the thousands of soldiers has a distinct facial expression. In 2007, workers in another part of China uncovered a mini clay army—several hundred soldiers almost 12 inches (30.5 cm) tall. They were made about 100 years after the larger terra-cotta soldiers.

SULFIDES & SULFATES

• SMELLY ELEMENT, MANY MINERALS •

Pee-yew! How rude!

It wasn't me!

A VOLCANO, JAVA, INDONESIA

FAST STATS: SULFUR

HARDNESS:
1.5–2.5

STREAK:
Colorless

LUSTER:
Greasy or resinous

What's the big stink about sulfur? It's easy to tell when it's nearby. This native element is famous for its smell—like that of rotten eggs. But it's also a key part of many minerals that are grouped into two classes: sulfides and sulfates, and some of these minerals are an important part of daily life.

DID YOU KNOW?
A SOOTHING SULFATE

If you have sore muscles, soaking in some water filled with Epsom salts—a form of a sulfate mineral—can ease the pain. This multipurpose mineral can also ease the itch caused by poison ivy or bug bites and help remove splinters.

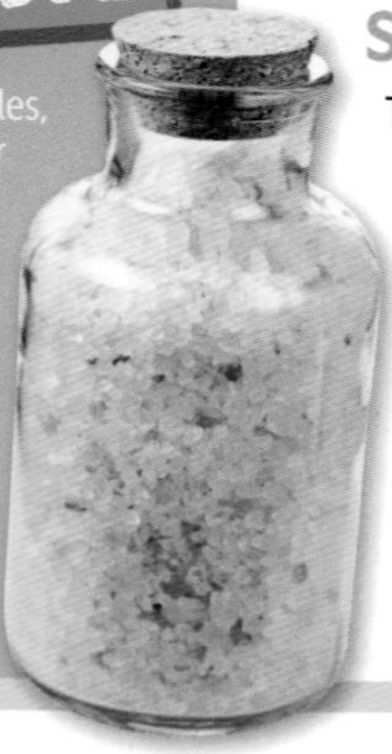

SOME MORE ORES

The sulfides are a combination of sulfur and a metal. Galena, for example, is a mixture of sulfur and lead, and the ore is a key source for the lead that turns up car batteries.

Sphalerite is another mineral that sees sulfur paired with a metal. This ore is the most important source of zinc, and zinc is one major metal. It's the fourth most commonly used metal in the world, and quite a brass act—combined with copper, it forms that shiny alloy.

Fooled ya!

Another important metal is molybdenum, and its major source is the sulfide molybdenite. Molybdenum is added to steel to make it stronger and more heat resistant.

One sulfide is well known for its trickery: pyrite. The most common of the sulfides, it has a shiny golden color that has led some people to mistake it for gold. That's given pyrite the nickname fool's gold (see page 105). Yet another sulfide is known for its smell. When you hit a chunk of arsenopyrite with a hammer, it smells like garlic. Don't even THINK about putting in on your pizza (or anything else), though: It also contains the element arsenic, which is poisonous!

THE HARD AND THE SOFT

Sulfur combined with oxygen and certain metal elements creates sulfate minerals. An important one for the steel industry is scheelite, a mineral that is a source of the metal tungsten. Like molybdenum, tungsten makes steel harder. And tungsten can really take the heat, so it's used inside many lightbulbs, which produce heat as well as light.

The most common sulfate mineral is gypsum. While scheelite is a 4.5 to 5 on the Mohs scale, gypsum rates only a 2. But don't let its softness fool you: Gypsum has important uses. You probably have some in your home, as many U.S. buildings have wallboard underneath the paint or wallpaper you see. That light board is made from gypsum.

EARLY RADIOS OFTEN USED A **GALENA CRYSTAL** TO HELP CONVERT THE RADIO SIGNAL **INTO AUDIO** PEOPLE COULD HEAR. SOME PEOPLE EVEN MADE THESE SIMPLE **RADIOS AT HOME.**

GYPSUM USED IN PLASTER

WHERE IN THE WORLD?
A WHOLE LOT OF GYPSUM

A desert in southern New Mexico, U.S.A., looks like a beach filled with fine white sand. Except it's not the type of quartz sand you would commonly find on a beach—it's gypsum. You can find this stretch of white mineral at White Sands National Monument, near Alamogordo. About 250 million years ago, the area was covered with a sea that was full of calcium, sulfur, and oxygen, the key chemical ingredients needed to make gypsum. Over millions of years, the water dried up, and chunks of gypsum were left behind. Millions more years later, the movement of tectonic plates in the region created mountains. Over time, rain and melted snow carried gypsum found on the mountains into a basin. Then, starting about 10,000 years ago, as temperatures rose and fell, the gypsum broke apart, and the wind carried this gypsum "sand" to where the national monument is today. The gypsum covers 275 square miles (712 sq km) and forms massive dunes that visitors can explore.

MINERALS & MONEY

• THE SMART MONEY IS ON MINERALS •

To coin a phrase, we'd be cashless without minerals. They make up the coins that jangle in your pocket, and they even turn up in paper bills. Here's a look at how our money relies on minerals.

THE FIRST U.S. COINS

Just a few years after the United States was formed, its leaders realized the country needed its own cold, hard cash. So in 1792, Congress created the U.S. Mint to make coins for the country. The first coins that were widely available were made of copper, with a value of 1.5 cents. These were soon followed by coins of silver and gold. Honoring the country's national bird, a gold coin worth $10 was called an eagle, and a half eagle was worth $5.

I am no more!

TWO NICKELS BETTER THAN ONE?

For many years, most U.S. coins were made of silver, gold, and copper. In 1865, however, an alloy with nickel in it was used to make a new five-cent coin that was soon called—surprise!—the nickel. But the mint was also still making silver half-dimes, which were also worth five cents. The two coins with the same value both circulated until 1873. That year, the last half-dimes were minted. But the nickel has lived on.

PAPER MONEY

Tiny metallic flakes are added to some of the ink used to print paper bills. They make the ink change color when the bill is tilted different ways in the light. This makes it impossible for someone to make a fake bill by copying one on a copier or using a computer scanner.

THE **FIRST COINS**, MADE OF A **MIXTURE OF** SILVER AND GOLD, WERE USED IN AN **ANCIENT KINGDOM CALLED LYDIA**, IN WHAT IS NOW TURKEY. THEY **APPEARED MORE THAN** 2,600 YEARS AGO.

You sayin' I'm old?

CHANGING THE FORMULA

At times, the U.S. government has messed with the metals in its coins. During World War II, the government needed copper and nickel to make military supplies. So, in 1943, pennies were made of steel coated with zinc instead of copper. And for most of the war, the nickel was made of an alloy of silver, copper, and manganese. Today, pennies are made almost entirely out of zinc, with just a little copper covering. The nickel still has nickel in it, but it's made mostly of copper. It can cost more to make a nickel—seven cents—than the coin is worth, so the government is considering adding zinc to the alloy to lower the cost. The government loses money minting pennies, too—each one costs almost two cents to make!

USING NICKEL MAKES SENSE

Scientists working for the aircraft maker Boeing found a new use for nickel. It's the main ingredient of an alloy that can be turned into one of the lightest and strongest metals known. Called a microlattice, the metal is made of super-tiny hollow tubes of the nickel alloy, but it's mostly air. A piece of the metal can sit on a puffy, white dandelion head and not crush it! In the future, the metal could be used to make lighter and stronger airplanes and spacecraft.

HALIDES
• SALTS OF THE EARTH •

There's no need to take this with a grain of salt—halides really are also called mineral salts. They are formed by a combination of metallic elements and one of these four elements: fluorine, chlorine, bromine, or iodine. Some of these minerals are pretty rare, but there's one exception: halite. You can eat it, use it to dry out wet things, wash with it, and spread it on icy roads. What's this miracle mineral? Sodium chloride—which you know as salt!

Look Ma, no cavities!

A GIFT FROM THE SEA

Like other halides, common salt, also called rock salt, is found in water. When the waters of ancient oceans dried up, rock salt was one of the minerals left behind. Today, it's mined in deposits that are deep underground and can be several thousand feet thick. Sometimes, mounds of salt rise up through underground rock layers, creating what are called salt domes. Pressure around the underlying salt, from tectonic movement or the weight of nearby rocks, can create these salt domes. The space between the top of the dome and the rocks around it sometimes holds pockets of oil or natural gas.

People don't just dig up old salt. They can also get it right from the sea. Salty water is trapped in shallow pools, and, eventually, the water dries up, leaving salt behind. Sea salt produced this way is often served in restaurants.

DRIED AND TRUE

Along with seasoning food, salt can be used to keep meats and other foods from going bad. How? Salt dries up water in foods. With less water, the bacteria that make the food rot can't do as much damage. Salt's drying power was useful in the past, too. Ancient Egyptians used salt to create mummies. A form of salt called natron was put into the dead bodies to remove all the moisture inside. As with food, this drying kept the body from rotting. Salt also formed some mummies naturally. In Iran, some miners who died in salt mines almost 2,000 years ago were turned into mummies.

SHINING BRIGHT

Another important halide is fluorite. Fluorite is the source of fluoride, a substance that fights tooth decay. Most toothpastes contain fluoride, and so do some mouth rinses. Some sharks are lucky—they don't have to brush to keep their teeth healthy because the outer part of their teeth is covered in fluoride, so they don't ever get cavities!

ROMAN SOLDIERS WERE SAID TO **GET SOME** OF THEIR **PAY IN SALT,** AND THE WORD **SALARY** COMES FROM *SAL,* THE **ROMAN WORD** FOR **SALT.**

WHERE IN THE WORLD? SALT CITY

People started mining salt in Wieliczka, Poland, more than 700 years ago. Today, the Wieliczka mine is a tourist attraction, where visitors descend 443 feet (135 m) underground, walk through tunnels carved out of the salt, see subterranean lakes, and explore 20 chambers, including a tavern and a museum. The most stunning salt chamber in Wieliczka is the Chapel of St. Kinga. It features art carved out of salt, and musicians sometimes play there. In 2000, one huge salt chamber in the mine was the site of the first underground balloon flight.

OXIDES & HYDROXIDES
• SOME OXCITING MINERALS •

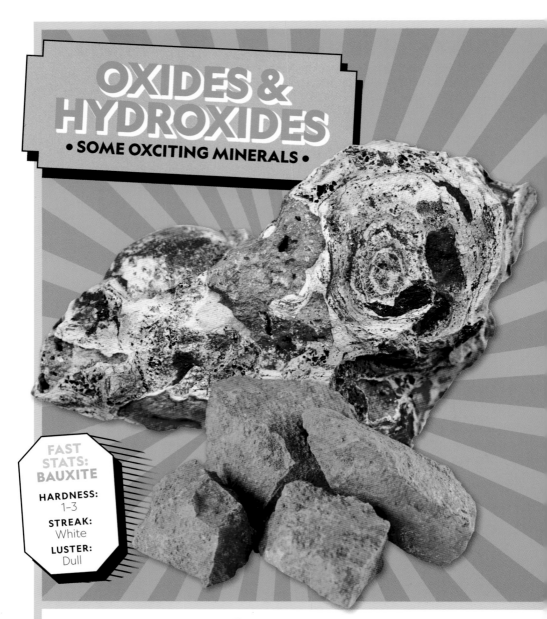

WHAT'S IN A NAME?

Bauxite comes from the French town Les Baux. The ore was first found there in 1821.

Oxygen—you might call it the essential element. It's in the air you breathe, the water you swim in, and the ground you walk on. And other elements love oxygen, as they pair with it to create lots of different compounds. These compounds include minerals that are grouped into two classes: Oxides are a combination of oxygen and metallic elements, and hydroxides form when hydrogen joins the party with these other elements. When water reacts with metals in rocks and minerals, a hydroxide is often the result.

METAL MANIA

Oxide ores give us many important metals. Different oxides contain most of the iron that's mined around the world. Ilmenite has some iron, but it's also the main source of titanium, a metal that is all around us, turning up in jewelry, scissors, and bicycle frames. Some people even have it in their bodies, as titanium is used to make some artificial joints. A form of titanium also gives white house paint its color. The metal is light and strong, so it ends up in aircraft engines and military equipment.

Another important oxide is chromite, the main source of chromium. This shiny silver metal is often used to cover parts of motorcycles and cars. The metal doesn't rust, and it makes those wheels gleam! Chromium is also added to steel and other metals to make them harder and resistant to heat. And a bright yellow paint that contained bits of chromium was once commonly used to paint school buses across the United States.

THE ORE THE MERRIER

Let's illuminate you about aluminum—it's the most common metal in Earth's crust, but it never appears alone. It occurs in ores, and its main source is bauxite. Technically, bauxite is a rock that's filled with many minerals, including the different hydroxides that give us aluminum. Most people know aluminum as the foil they use to wrap up leftovers, but the light and strong metal has many uses. It's in food and beverage cans, pots and pans, airplanes, and mirrors, among other products. Some of the world's tallest building have aluminum frames. Tiny bits of aluminum are also used in fireworks; they make the colorful explosions bright.

Getting aluminum out of bauxite and other ores is difficult, and at one time the metal was extremely expensive. During the 19th century, French ruler Napoleon III had special aluminum plates and utensils: Only he and his most important guests used them, and everyone else had to use the cheap stuff ... made from gold and silver! Aluminum became much easier to make by the end of that century. A new process using large amounts of electricity made it cheaper to remove aluminum from bauxite.

ONE ALUMINUM ALLOY IS SO STRONG THAT A WIRE MADE FROM IT COULD LIFT A FULLY LOADED TRACTOR TRAILER TRUCK!

Only the best for *moi*

MINES OF THE WORLD
• DIGGING DEEP FOR MINERALS •

To get the rocks and ores that produce the minerals the world needs, companies sometimes dig deep into the ground. Other times, their mines are on Earth's surface, in what are called open pits. Here's a look at some of the largest and most important mines and some of the equipment that makes mining easier.

GARZWEILER MINE, GERMANY

In the quest for coal, a German mining company has set up the world's largest mining operation. Garzweiler II, in the western part of Germany, covers an area of 18.5 square miles (48 sq km). Some parts of the mine are 650 feet (198 m) deep. The coal produced there, called lignite, helps provide some of Germany's electricity. (The country is one of the world's top producers of lignite.) In the future, when mining stops at Garzweiler II, water from the Rhine River may be used to fill the hole. If that happens, it will create Germany's third largest lake.

KIRUNA MINE, SWEDEN

People are on the move at the world's largest underground iron mine. Parts of the village of Kiruna, Sweden, buildings and all, are being moved as mining goes on at this iron giant. There's a risk that the ground around the town could give way and that everything in the community could fall into a hole. The move of buildings and people began in 2017 and could go on for 20 years or more.

BINGHAM CANYON MINE, UTAH

At more than three-quarters of a mile (1.2 km) deep and 2.5 miles (4 km) wide, the Bingham Canyon mine near Salt Lake City, Utah, U.S.A., is one of the world's deepest open-pit mines. It's so big that astronauts orbiting Earth on the International Space Station can see it from about 200 miles (322 km) above Earth. For more than 100 years, the mine has been one of the most productive in the world. To get the ore containing metals, miners blow up rock using 1,200 pounds (544 kg) of explosives at a time.

GRASBERG GOLD MINE, INDONESIA

Looking for lots of gold and copper in one place? Then head to the Grasberg mine in Indonesia, on the western side of the island of New Guinea. It is the world's second largest copper mine, and only three other mines in the world produce more gold. Most of Grasberg's mining used to take place in an open pit, but now most takes place underground. As of 2018, the metals still to be mined were worth about $14 billion.

MPONENG GOLD MINE, SOUTH AFRICA

Gold often forms deep within Earth, and getting at it can require digging one big hole. The Mponeng gold mine, near Johannesburg, South Africa, plunges 2.5 miles (4 km), making it one of the deepest holes ever dug by humans. How deep is deepest? Well, you could stack 10 Empire State Buildings on top of one another in this hole! At its deepest, the mine reaches temperatures of 140°F (60°C), so a mixture of ice and salt is sent down to help cool the miners, who—to reach the bottom—must take an hour-long elevator ride.

145

RECYCLING FACTS

• USING TWICE IS NICE •

The minerals in many of the products we use are so valuable that it would be a shame to waste them. That's why governments around the world encourage people to recycle, so that the materials can be used again. Recycling a material can be cheaper and use less energy and natural resources than making it from scratch. And because some metals can be dangerous, keeping them out of landfills reduces the chances of polluting water and soil.

 ① STEEL

Recycling one ton (.91 t) of steel saves:

- 2,500 pounds (1,134 kg) of iron ore
- 1,400 pounds (635 kg) of coal
- 120 pounds (54 kg) of limestone

② PLASTICS

Minerals used in plastics include talc, silica, clay, mica, and calcium carbonate.

- Recycling a ton (.91 t) of plastic saves 685 gallons (2,593 L) of oil.
- Lined up end-to-end, all the plastic thrown away each year could circle Earth four times.
- More than 25 percent of the materials recycling plants receive are plastics.
- Recycling five plastic bottles creates enough fiber to make one square foot (.09 sq m) of carpeting. Recycling 10 bottles creates enough fiber to make a T-shirt. Recycling 63 bottles creates enough fiber to make a sweater.

③ ALUMINUM

- Each year, Americans throw away more than $700 million in aluminum cans.

- Recycling aluminum uses just 5 percent of the energy needed to make new aluminum.

④ GLASS MADE FROM SAND

- Recycling glass saves 25–30 percent more energy than making new glass.

- About 80 percent of recycled glass is turned into new glass. Recycled glass also goes into fiberglass, some paving and landscaping materials, and new glass containers.

⑤ METALS IN ELECTRONICS

Many different metals go into our televisions, smartphones, computers, and other electronics. Each year, the world produces more than 53.5 million tons (48.5 t) of this "e-waste."

Recycling one million cellphones would recover:

- 20,000 pounds (9,072 kg) of copper
- 550 pounds (250 kg) of silver
- 50 pounds (23 kg) of gold
- 20 pounds (9 kg) of palladium

Always recycle!

PAY DIRT!

Recycling one million laptop computers would save enough energy to power about 3,500 U.S. homes for one year.

CARBONATES
• FROM SHELLS TO STATUES •

DOLOMITE

MALACHITE

FAST STATS: CALCITE

HARDNESS:
3

STREAK:
White

LUSTER:
Vitreous

Pretty cool!

What do oyster shells and marble statues have in common? They both contain a form of carbonate, one of the major groups of minerals. Carbonates are a mixture of oxygen and carbon, along with a metallic element. Carbonates are often found in seawater or where ancient oceans once covered the land. They can appear in all three types of rocks.

Shell we dance?

CARBONATE STARS

The most common carbonate is calcite. It's the mineral found in both oyster and some other seashells and in marble. It's also in limestone, and since marble and limestone are used to make a lot of public buildings, you might find yourself at a lot of calcite sites. You're also surrounded by calcite when you enter a cave filled with stalactites or stalagmites, as it's one of the minerals that forms these pointy shapes. Calcite is also added to some food for animals, to paint to make it white, and to some household cleaning products.

Similar to calcite is dolomite, which has the same chemicals in it as calcite, with a little magnesium thrown in. Dolomite is the main mineral of the rock dolostone, which is also called dolomite rock. This rock, like limestone, is often used in construction. It's crushed and added to concrete and asphalt, among other products.

A colorful example of a carbonate is malachite. A bit of copper in it makes the mineral green. Malachite was once a major source of that metal, but now most is mined from other ores. But malachite has still proved itself useful, mostly in art. Crushed into a powder, it makes a green paint. Solid pieces of malachite have been used in jewelry.

ROCKS IN YOUR NOGGIN

This might make your head spin: You have tiny calcium carbonate crystals in your inner ear that help you keep your balance. The little stones, called otoconia, sit in a gel that's in small sacs called the utricle and saccule. When we move our heads, the crystals move and spark nearby cells that send signals to the brain. These signals help the brain figure out how much the head is moving. But if the crystals fall out of their sacs and into nearby tubes called canals, that sets the brain into a tizzy and makes you feel dizzy. The dislodged fragments make the brain think the head is moving when it isn't, creating a spinning sensation called vertigo. The spinning sensation usually stops in under a minute, and special head movements can help return the crystals to where they belong.

WHERE IN THE WORLD? A GREEN SCENE

Malachite was once mined in great quantities in Russia, and some of that green mineral decorates St. Isaac's Cathedral, one of the most famous buildings in St. Petersburg. It features columns of malachite. The mineral also was used in mosaics, artworks made up of different small stones. Altogether 16 tons (14.5 t) of the mineral were used inside the building.

PHOSPHATES
• A COLORFUL GROUP •

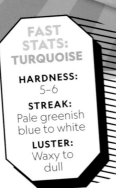

ick almost any color of the rainbow, and there's likely to be phosphate mineral that matches it. Phosphates contain a mixture of the elements phosphorous and oxygen, along with a metal. Because they have similar crystal structures, this group also includes minerals known as arsenates—think arsenic—and vanadates.

A FABULOUS PHOSPHATE

Across the world, people discovered the phosphate turquoise, and they fell in love with its light blue-green color. The mineral gets this color from small amounts of copper. For several thousand years, it's been mined for gems that turn up in all kinds of jewelry and pieces of art. Turquoise was especially important to native people of North and Central America, including the Aztec, of what is today Mexico—they thought the mineral was more valuable than silver or gold. American Indians of the south-western United States also value turquoise, and it's still commonly used there for jewelry.

No bones about it!

AN APPETITE FOR APATITE

Chew on this: When you're eating your favorite food, the phosphate apatite helps you enjoy it. This mineral is the most common phosphate, and it's found in the teeth of many animals, including humans. Apatite is actually the name for several related minerals, and most of it is crushed up and used as fertilizer. But one form of it helps in medicine after someone has a limb removed: It is used to fill in holes in the remaining bone. Apatite can also help bone grow into new, artificial limbs that some people receive after operations. This new growth helps join together the old bone and the new limb.

WHAT'S IN A NAME?

"Turquoise" comes from a French word meaning "Turkish stone." The gemstones first reached Europe from traders who transported them through Turkey.

TOUGH STUFF

One of the vanadates is vanadinite, a rare mineral that is the main source of the metal vanadium. It helps make steel stronger and lighter, and it's been doing this for decades. In 1908, carmaker Henry Ford used vanadium to make his Model T stronger than other cars on the road. The Ford car was cheaper, too, and over the years, vanadium was used to make 15 million Model Ts!

LARGE **BATTERIES** MADE WITH A **FORM OF VANADIUM** ARE SOMETIMES USED TO **STORE ENERGY** CREATED FROM THE SUN AND WIND.

SOLAR CONTAINER UNIT

ORGANIC "MINERALS"
• IT'S ALIVE! SORT OF ... •

I'm picture pearl-fect

When is a mineral not a mineral? When it comes from something alive—or that was once alive. Geologists say minerals are solids made of inorganic material—that means they're not living or produced by a living creature. But there are some hard substances found in nature that are produced by living things. Here's a look at some of the common non-minerals often found in nature.

FROM LIVING PLANTS TO POWER PLANTS

Hundreds of millions of years ago, parts of the world were covered with huge swamps. When plants died, they sank into the water. Over time, more dead plants piled up in the water. Then, sand and silt and clay filled the swamps, forming sedimentary rocks that pressed down

Open wide!

on the remains of the dead plants. With the pressure, some chemical changes, and a lot of time, the dead plants became coal.

When people began digging up coal, they realized it burned and could be a source of heat. Coal is a fossil fuel—a natural fuel formed from the remains of something that was once alive. Today, most coal is used to create steam in power plants, which then spins turbines that generate electricity. Some coal is also heated to create coke—not the soft drink, but rather a source of fuel used to make some metals. And a form of coal called jet comes from ancient trees and is often cut into gemstones.

Coal contains the element carbon, and so do diamonds. For that reason, some people have thought that diamonds come from coal. After all, Superman sometimes uses his super strength to squeeze the black rock to make a shiny diamond. But outside of comics, coal is *not* the source of diamonds.

TREASURES FROM THE SEA

If a little bit of sand gets in your shoe, you probably get a little irritated, take off your shoe, and shake it out. When an oyster or mussel gets some sand in its shell, it gets irritated, too. But these shellfish, called mollusks, don't get rid of the irritant. Instead, they cover the sand or other particles with a natural substance they make called nacre. Over time, layers of nacre produce the organic gem we call a pearl. Top-notch natural pearls are hard to find and expensive to collect. Most pearls today are cultured, which means people raise the shellfish and add the "seed" that will become a pearl.

Hard coral is another organic material that seems like a rock or mineral. But it's actually the skeleton of a tiny sea creature called a polyp. The polyp creates an exoskeleton—a hard outer covering—as it takes the compound calcium carbonate out of the water that surrounds it. Large stretches of coral form reefs that become home to many fish.

MOTHER NACRE

The nacre inside mollusks is also called mother-of-pearl. Scientists sometimes call this material a biomineral—a mineral made by a living thing. Mollusks take calcium carbonate in seawater and create the mineral aragonite to form their nacre. For several thousand years, humans have removed the mother-of-pearl from shellfish and found many uses for it. It's been turned into buttons and used to decorate furniture. Nacre is very strong, and scientists are exploring ways to create a synthetic version in their labs. This human-made nacre could be used to make artificial teeth and bones or superstrong building materials.

IT TAKES A LAYER OF **DEAD PLANTS** **50 FEET** (15 M) **THICK** TO PRODUCE A LAYER OF **COAL** **FIVE FEET** (1.5 M) **THICK.**

GEMS
• MINERAL BEAUTY •

As humans discovered minerals and their many uses, some people had a gem of an idea. Pieces of some of the most colorful or shiny minerals could be cut and polished to make jewelry. These pieces worn around the neck or in rings are called gemstones, or gems for short.

Isn't that precious

Jewelers measure the value of a diamond based on four traits, called the 4 Cs. These are commonly applied to diamonds, but other gemstones are judged the same way.

- **CUT:** Some gems are a cut above, based on how well they were cut from the larger pieces of mineral that produced them. Jewelers look for gems that are balanced and for each side, called a facet, to reflect light evenly.

- **COLOR:** Facets are important for determining a gem's color, as light enters the gem through them. And it's light that helps determine the exact color people see when they admire a gem. Each gem has a range of colors, with some shades more desirable than others.

- **CLARITY:** It's clear to see the value of clarity. A perfect gemstone won't have inclusions—tiny bits of material that got trapped inside the mineral as it formed. It also shouldn't have any scratches on the surface. Inclusions or scratches reduce the gem's clarity.

- **CARAT:** The purity of gold is measured in karats, and gems are weighed in carats. C the difference? The size of a gem is determined by its weight, and one carat equals .007 ounce (0.2 g). Larger examples of a particular gem are more expensive not just because of their size. Finding big samples of a mineral that can be cut into a gem is much harder than finding smaller ones.

Of the thousands of known minerals, only about 130 are used to make gems. And among these, some are more popular than others. Jewelry with gems can cost millions of dollars if the gems are rare, particularly large, or especially beautiful. The most valuable gems are called precious gems, a group that includes diamonds, sapphires, rubies, and emeralds. Other gems that are more common, but still beautiful, are called semiprecious.

Not all gems come from minerals. A few, such as amber and pearls, come from organic sources. And scientists have learned how to duplicate many gems in their labs using chemicals and heat. That's useful when a gem is expensive, like a diamond. Synthetic diamonds allow people to enjoy the sparkle without the expensive price tag. Synthetic diamonds and other gems are also used in industry. Synthetic sapphires, for example, are used to make a scratch-resistant "glass" for some watch faces.

BERYL-ING ALONG

The mineral beryl bears some attention. It's one of the few minerals that produces a variety of gemstones, depending on their color. Beryl is a silicate mineral, and it is a source of the metal beryllium, used to make several kinds of alloys. Green beryl, called emerald, gets its color from the elements chromium and vanadium. Only beryl with the deepest shades of green are called emerald (see page 158). The semiprecious gemstone aquamarine also comes from beryl. It gets its light bluish green color from iron (see page 124). A pink form of beryl is called morganite. It's named for the 19th-century American banker J. P. Morgan, one of the richest men in the country, who was also a mineral collector. Beryl also produces gemstones that are yellow, red, and dark blue—and one with no color at all!

DIAMONDS
• THE GLITTERING GEM •

Diamonds are forever, the saying goes. Of all the world's gemstones, these "rocks" are probably the most popular—and usually the most expensive. Here's a look at some of the world's most famous diamonds.

① THE HOPE DIAMOND

You can hope all you want, but you'll never get to wear the Hope Diamond. You can, however, see it on display at the Smithsonian Museum of Natural History in Washington, D.C. The 45.52 carat diamond is part of a necklace that contains several dozen smaller diamonds. The Hope is blue, the rarest color for a diamond, and the largest one of its kind. It's also been said to be cursed because at least one of its previous owners met an untimely end. But most of the superstitions surrounding the giant gem just aren't true. The Hope Diamond is considered priceless, but one estimate puts it at a quarter of a billion dollars.

GREAT GEMS

In 2018, a Canadian mining company uncovered the largest diamond ever found in North America, weighing in at a whopping 552 carats.

② CULLINAN DIAMOND

When it comes to big diamonds, the Cullinan is the all-time whopper. At more than 3,100 carats—or about 1.3 pounds (0.6 kg)—it was the largest gem-quality diamond ever unearthed. Discovered in South Africa in 1905, it was soon cut into nine major gems and many smaller ones. The largest of the polished diamonds is the Star of Africa, weighing in at 530 carats. That makes it the largest colorless cut diamond in the world.

By Jove!

③ THE PINK STAR DIAMOND

Pink diamonds are among the rarest in the world, and one of them is a record setter. In 2017, the Pink Star diamond, weighing almost 60 carats, sold for just over $71 million dollars—the highest price ever paid at an auction for any kind of gemstone.

④ AZATURE BLACK DIAMOND NAIL POLISH

In 2012, if you wanted to have the world's most expensive fingernails, all you had to do was buy a bottle of Azature black diamond nail polish. Or, rather, *the* bottle, since the company made only one. The polish contained 267 carats of black diamonds and sold for $250,000! The next year, the company went diamond dizzy when it introduced a new polish with white gems. The price: $1 million! Azature still offers polish with much less diamond in it that sells for $25.

That's nuts!

⑤ PEANUT BUTTER

In 2014, geologist Dan Frost turned peanut butter into a diamond. Yes, you read that right: *peanut butter*. In his lab, he used high heat and extreme pressure to turn the carbon in the gooey food into a tiny diamond. Carbon, the only element in diamonds, turns up in all the foods we eat (except salt), including eggs, cheese—and peanut butter. Frost's process takes weeks to make even tiny diamonds, however.

THE EYE OF BRAHMA, A RARE BLACK DIAMOND, IS SAID TO BE CURSED BECAUSE SOMEONE ONCE STOLE IT FROM THE STATUE OF A HINDU GOD.

EMERALDS

• THE GREAT GREEN GEM •

GREAT GEMS

One famous Colombian stone is the Chalk Emerald, named for the last person who owned it. A beautiful 37.8-carat gem sits in the middle of a ring, surrounded by tiny diamonds. The ring is now on display at the Smithsonian Museum of Natural History.

If you're lucky enough to own an emerald, your friends might turn green with envy. Emeralds are the most valued green gems in the world. In the best condition, they can be worth more than some diamonds. Emeralds can turn up in any of the three major kinds of rocks, but they are rare. And not all green beryl is good enough to be an emerald. Only the darkest green of the gems make the grade. Many emeralds also have inclusions on their surface, so they can break apart fairly easily.

GOING FOR THE GREEN

The ancient Egyptians mined emeralds starting about 2,500 years ago. For a time, the Romans controlled Egypt, and emeralds from there have survived in Roman jewelry. Starting about 1,500 years ago, the native people of Colombia worked several large emerald mines and traded their green gems to places as far away as what is today Mexico. The Aztec called the gem *quetzalitzi*, named for the quetzal, a bird with bright green feathers.

We're a big deal

When the Spanish reached Mexico, the Aztec gave them some of their emerald jewelry. The Spanish found the Colombian mines soon after, and they took the emeralds and traded them around the world. They turn up in jewelry and art in Asia and the Middle East. The Colombian gems are a deeper color and have greater clarity than emeralds from most other mines.

It's not that easy being green

BLING RING

In 2017, the Harry Winston jewelry company paid $5.5 million for the Rockefeller Emerald—a stone weighing just over 18 carats—breaking the world record for price paid per carat for an emerald sold at auction.

THE **OLDEST** KNOWN EMERALDS, FOUND IN **SOUTH AFRICA**, ARE ALMOST **THREE BILLION** YEARS OLD.

AQUAMARINE

• WOO HOO—THIS STONE'S BLUE •

WHAT'S IN A NAME?

"Aquamarine" comes from the Latin words for "sea water."

You could say that aquamarines and emeralds are gemstone cousins, since they're both a type of beryl. While aquamarines aren't as valuable or rare as the green gem, they tend to have fewer inclusions than emeralds. That gives the bluish green stone a look like glass.

SOME **EARLY EYEGLASSES** USED **TINY BITS** OF AQUAMARINE FOR THE **LENSES.**

Lens partyyy

Aquamarine can also form gigantic crystals. One of the largest was almost 243 pounds (110 kg)—just a bit more than the weight of some newborn African elephants! As with emeralds, the deeper the color, the more desirable the aquamarine. Before they're sold for jewelry, some aquamarines are heated, which makes them a darker shade of blue.

I'm cuter than any gem

PEAK PERFORMANCE

For miners in Pakistan's Karakoram Mountains, mining aquamarine is a real blast—of dynamite, that is. While some miners go deep into the planet to get minerals, the Pakistanis go *up* about 15,000 feet (4,572 m) to find aquamarines and other gems. To get the gems, miners bring explosives with them up the mountains and set them off in the rocks. They rely on horses and donkeys to bring their supplies up the steep mountainsides.

WHERE IN THE WORLD? A CUT ABOVE

Brazil is home to many of the world's best aquamarine mines. One of them, found in the state of Minas Gerais, produced the world's largest cut aquamarine, standing 14 inches (36 cm) tall and weighing more than 10,300 carats. The gem is called the Dom Pedro, and it has a history. When it was taken from the mine during the 1980s, the Dom Pedro was part of a massive aquamarine crystal that weighed nearly 100 pounds (45 kg). But then—oops! The miners dropped the crystal, and it broke into three pieces. The two smaller pieces were cut up into many gemstones, but the largest remained whole. Then, a German artist spent six months turning the rough crystal into what's really a stone sculpture, not a gemstone for someone to wear. It's named for the first two emperors of Brazil, who ruled during the 19th century. Today, Dom Pedro sits in the Smithsonian Museum of Natural History in Washington, D.C., U.S.A., not far from the Hope Diamond.

RUBIES & SAPPHIRES

• SEEING RED—AND BLUE •

Lady in re-d-d-d-d

Blinded by beauty

Rubies are red, sapphires are blue, and if you own these gemstones, well, lucky you! They are two of the most prized gems in the world, and some rubies are more valuable than diamonds of the same size.

Beryl isn't the only mineral that makes several valuable gems. Corundum, one of the hardest minerals on the planet, is often used as an abrasive—a material that can make rough things smooth. It's also the source of these two gems. The element chromium gives rubies their red color, whereas small amounts of iron and

CORUNDUM THAT DOESN'T HAVE ANY COLOR IS CALLED **WHITE** SAPPHIRE. THIS GEM IS SOMETIMES USED IN **ENGAGEMENT RINGS,** SINCE THEY'RE LESS EXPENSIVE THAN THE MORE TRADITIONAL DIAMOND.

SLIP INTO SOME RUBY SHOES

In the movie *The Wizard of Oz,* when Dorothy clicks her heels to go home, she is wearing a pair of ruby slippers. Using real rubies would have been too expensive, though. So the shoes were covered with tiny, shiny discs called sequins. But in 1989, the jeweler Harry Winston created *real* ruby shoes that look like the ones Dorothy wore. They feature 4,600 rubies, along with some diamonds, and are worth $3 million!

titanium provide the color for sapphires. Like other colored gemstones, the darkest ones of each of these are the most valuable. Corundum can also produce gems of other colors, such as pink or yellow, and these are called fancy sapphires.

In the ancient Indian language of Sanskrit, a ruby is called *ratnaraj,* which means "the king of gems." Sapphires, though, have often been popular with royalty, turning up in crowns and in jewelry. Princess Diana of Great Britain wore a sapphire engagement ring, and later, her son Prince William gave the ring to his wife, Catherine, Duchess of Cambridge.

Click, click

GEMS FROM THE LAB

Like some other gemstones, rubies and sapphires are sometimes made in labs. These synthetic gems turn up in jewelry, but they also have other uses. The synthetic rubies are sometimes used to make lasers that remove unwanted tattoos. Plates of clear synthetic sapphires cover the scanners at the grocery store checkout line. And when you check your email on a smartphone, the screen might be covered with a layer of synthetic sapphire.

ROCK STAR
A STAR STONE

In 1938, when Roy Spencer spotted a large black rock near his home in Queensland, Australia, he didn't know what he had found. He took it home to show his father, who initially deemed it a worthless crystal. By some accounts, the Spencers even used it as a doorstop!

About 10 years later, a jeweler who sometimes bought sapphires from Mr. Spencer stopped by. When Roy fetched the rock to show him, the jeweler realized that the young Aussie had found a rare black sapphire. Impurities in the gem had created what looked like a six-pointed star inside. The jeweler bought Roy's find and cut and polished it to create the Black Star of Queensland, a 733-carat gem, making it one of the largest sapphires in the world. At one time, the former doorstop was valued at just over $4 million.

CROWN JEWELS & FAMOUS COLLECTIONS

• SOME CROWNING ACHIEVEMENTS •

What's one way to show the world how rich and powerful you are? Wear expensive gems in your crown, around your neck, or on your clothes! For several thousand years, rulers have bought—and showed off—their gems. And as people who weren't royalty started bringing home the big bucks, they bought gem-covered jewelry, too. Here's a look at some of the world's great gem and jewelry collections.

IMPERIAL CROWN OF THE HOLY ROMAN EMPIRE

Other European royalty also once sported some pretty impressive bling. Austria no longer has a king or queen, but it was once ruled by an emperor. Vienna's Imperial Treasury has a golden emperor's crown that's more than 1,000 years old. Covering it are pearls, rubies, amethysts, and other gems.

GOLDEN JUBILEE DIAMOND

Some Asian rulers also have crown jewels, and the ones for Thailand's royalty include the Golden Jubilee diamond. This brown gem was discovered in the 1980s, and the cut version is just under 546 carats, making it the largest cut diamond in the world.

I'm loaded!

ELIZABETH TAYLOR DIAMOND

Kings and queens aren't the only people who go gaga for gems. Anyone with enough money and a love for jewelry can flaunt their wealth with gemstones. The most valuable private collection sold at auction to date belonged to American film actress Elizabeth Taylor. In 2011, her diamonds, pearls, emeralds, and gold sold for just over $137 million. The collection included a diamond ring that sold for almost $9 million.

IMPERIAL STATE CROWN

Another notable item in the British crown jewels collection is the Imperial State Crown. It's made from gold, silver, and platinum, and its gems include more than 2,800 diamonds, 17 sapphires, and 11 emeralds. One of the diamonds came from the same rock that produced the Star of Africa.

SOVEREIGN'S SCEPTER

Through the centuries, kings and queens have amassed some of the greatest gem collections, often called crown jewels. In the United Kingdom, the crown jewels are on display in the Tower of London. One of these items is the Sovereign's Scepter. A scepter is a rod used by a ruler as a symbol of the ruler's authority; it is often topped with gems or precious metals. The Sovereign's Scepter features Cullinan I, also called the Star of Africa, the largest cut white diamond in the world.

Now that's a workout!

GREAT GEMS

One of the crowns in the Tower of London collection could be a royal pain in the neck to wear for too long—it weighs almost five pounds (2.3 kg)!

165

JADE
• MADE IN THE JADE •

You green with envy?

WHAT'S IN A NAME?

"Jade" came from the Spanish expression *piedra de ijada*, which means "stone for the side." When they reached Central America, the Spanish saw the local people sometimes holding a piece of jade against their side, since it was said to cure kidney pain.

Tough enough to be used as an ax, beautiful enough to be worn as jewelry—those are the two sides of jade. What's sold as jade today actually comes from one of two different minerals—jadeite and nephrite. Jadeite is a compound that includes aluminum, while nephrite contains magnesium, among other elements. The two minerals are so alike, it took until the 1860s to discover that what was called jade actually came from both jadeite and nephrite.

Most people think of jade as green, and the color comes from some iron in the chemical mix. Jadeite, though, is white in its pure form, and jade can appear in shades of yellow and purple.

We're jade for each other

CHINA'S CHOICE GEM

Starting in the Stone Age, people around the world shaped jade into weapons and tools. They also carved it into small art objects and polished it to make gemstones. But no country cherished jade as much as China, where it was sometimes called "the stone of heaven." The written symbol for jade in Chinese is almost 5,000 years old, but people were making items out of it for hundreds of years before then. Along with tools and art, jade was used to make musical instruments, such as gongs and flutes.

For centuries, only China's rulers and the wealthiest families could own this cherished gem. The Chinese thought that jade could keep away evil spirits and bring long life.

Starting in the 1700s, Chinese carvers realized that a new kind of jade coming from outside the country made better statues and jewelry. The new jade was jadeite, and it became the preferred source for jade art. Today, it is still preferred over nephrite.

ONE BIG BUDDHA

The Buddha, founder of one of the world's major religions, Buddhism, lived in Nepal and India more than 2,500 years ago. His teachings became popular in China, too, so it seems right that a giant Buddha statue would be carved out of jade. But not just any Buddha—this one is the Jade Buddha for Universal Peace. The Buddha was cut from a single block of rare jade from Canada; at 19.8 tons (18 t), it is believed to be the largest piece of gem-quality jade ever found. The Buddha—standing eight feet (2.4 m) tall and weighing in at 4.4 tons (4 t)—was completed in Thailand in 2008. Like a true "rock" star, it toured the world, going on display in more than 120 cities in 20 countries. Today, the Jade Buddha is on permanent display in Bendigo, Australia, at a Buddhist temple.

MAGICAL & MYSTERIOUS MINERALS
• PRETTY POWER TOOLS •

Gems dazzle people with their beauty. But as you've heard before, some people have long thought certain gems have special powers, including the ability to heal the sick and protect people from bad luck. Here are some of the gems said to be more than just a pretty stone for someone to wear.

1 MOONSTONE

Moonstone is a gem-quality version of two feldspar minerals that seems to glow from the inside. In some parts of Asia, it's thought to be a good-luck charm, and it's said to make people calm. To some, moonstone was a boon for people seeking true love. They were told to hold on to a moonstone during a full moon and picture the person they wanted to be with. Then, the love seekers had to carry the moonstone with them until the next full moon, and their true love would appear.

Such beauty!

2 ROSE QUARTZ

Of course, even true love can go bad, and that's when you might need some rose quartz. The pink variety of this mineral is said to cure a broken heart. Some people once claimed it could help people deal with all sorts of disappointment, not just the loss of love. Ancient Egyptians believed wearing rose quartz helped to keep people from growing old.

③ MALACHITE

Malachite was once thought to have protective and healing powers. Parents in some parts of Europe placed the gem near their child's bed to keep away evil spirits. Some merchants wore malachite, thinking it could bring them good luck in their business.

④ AQUAMARINE

If sailors wanted to have a long life, they may have kept some aquamarine handy. Ancient Romans believed that aquamarine was sacred to Neptune, their god of the sea, and sailors thought it could protect them while they were oceangoing. The gem was also thought to calm rough waters.

Don't try this at home!

⑤ EMERALD

In ancient times, people seeking to predict the future sometimes put emeralds under their tongues. This was just one of the special powers claimed for this green gem. It was also said to improve people's memory, help them speak better, and cure certain diseases.

⑥ SAPPHIRE

Another gem said to have calming powers was sapphire. But instead of smoothing the sea, it could smooth out rough relations between people. Ancient rulers sometimes wore sapphires to protect them from danger.

My preciousss

169

BIRTHSTONES
• GEM OF THE MONTH •

When something's a dime a dozen, that means it's pretty common and cheap. But there's nothing cheap about birthstones. There are 12 in all, one for each month of the year. Where did the idea of birthstones come from? No one knows for sure, but starting a few hundred years ago, people began to associate each month with a stone. People born in that month were said to have special personality traits linked to their stone. And birthstones were thought to have healing powers. In 1912, a group of American jewelers created the list of modern birthstones. Today, jewelry with these gems make popular gifts.

JANUARY
GEM: Garnet
PERSONALITY TRAIT: Loyalty
HEALING POWER: Strengthens heart and lungs

FEBRUARY
GEM: Amethyst
PERSONALITY TRAIT: Sincerity
HEALING POWER: Reduces pain and improves blood circulation

MARCH
GEM: Aquamarine
PERSONALITY TRAIT: Courage
HEALING POWER: Helps the liver, throat, and other parts of the body

APRIL
GEM: Diamond
PERSONALITY TRAIT: Enduring love
HEALING POWER: General healing of the sick

MAY
GEM: Emerald
PERSONALITY TRAIT: Love and success
HEALING POWER: Strengthens heart, lungs, and other body parts

JUNE
GEM: Pearl
PERSONALITY TRAIT: Lasting love
HEALING POWER: Cures stomach ailments and skin problems

JULY

GEM: Ruby

PERSONALITY TRAIT:
Contentment

HEALING POWER:
Fights infections and calms
the mind

AUGUST

GEM: Peridot

PERSONALITY TRAIT:
Happiness

HEALING POWER:
Slows the aging process,
reduces stress, fights fevers

SEPTEMBER

GEM: Sapphire

PERSONALITY TRAIT:
Clear thinking

HEALING POWER:
Reduces pain and
strengthens the
nervous system

Call me hope-al

OCTOBER

GEM: Opal

PERSONALITY TRAIT: Hope

HEALING POWER:
Strengthens the kidney and helps
with women's health

NOVEMBER

GEM: Topaz

PERSONALITY TRAIT:
Faithfulness

HEALING POWER:
Balances emotions
and strengthens the liver

DECEMBER

GEM: Turquoise

PERSONALITY TRAIT: Success

HEALING POWER: Cures
headaches and earaches, among
other ailments

TOURMALINE
• THE RAINBOW ROCK •

Looks can be deceiving, as Portuguese explorers found out almost 500 years ago. They thought the green and red gems they discovered in Brazil were emeralds and rubies. Nope. The colorful stones were all tourmalines.

No matter your favorite color, you can probably find a tourmaline to match it. You can also see tourmalines with several colors in one gem ... or with no color at all! Tourmalines come in more colors and mixtures of colors than any other gem. The Egyptians called it rainbow rock, and there's nothing quite like it under the rainbow.

MANY MINERALS, ONE GEM

Eye of the tiger

Tourmaline is actually the name for 32 different silicate minerals that contain boron and other elements. These minerals have the same crystal structure, but some of the chemicals in them are different, and they look different, too. Tourmalines usually form in igneous rocks called pegmatites, along with granite. Some are also found in metamorphic rocks such as gneiss.

The three most common tourmaline minerals are schorl, elbaite, and dravite. Schorl is black and the most common of all. In England during the late 1800s, people sometimes wore schorl jewelry after a loved one died, since wearing black showed they were mourning their loss. Elbaite is the most colorful of the minerals and produces most of the tourmaline sold as gems. One elbaite mine can produce gems of many different colors. Dravite comes in shades of brown or dark yellow, and it sometimes mixes with another mineral of the same "family": uvite.

CAT GOT YOUR GEM?

For feline lovers, tourmalines may be the cat's meow. After some elbaite tourmalines are cut into gems, a line of light shines through the center of them. This effect is called a cat's eye, since some people think the gem looks a little like, well, a cat's eye. The effect happens with some other gems, too. The tourmalines and other stones that have a cat's eye are called cabochons. They are rounded and highly polished, without the notable facets most gemstones have. The line comes from light reflecting off tiny mineral fibers inside the gem that are arranged in parallel lines. The line that appears in the rock can shift about. The movement comes when the light source above the gem moves, if the rock moves under the light, or if a person looking at the gem moves his or her head. Sounds like the purrfect way to entertain a cat.

A TOURMALINE WITH **GREEN** AROUND ITS EDGES AND A RED CENTER IS CALLED A **WATERMELON.**

WHERE IN THE WORLD? MAINE'S MAIN MINERAL

Spotting a glint of green, Elijah Hamlin and Ezekiel Holmes made history. In 1820, the two men were searching for minerals on Mount Mica in Paris, Maine, U.S.A. The green they saw came from tourmaline, though the men didn't know this at the time. They also couldn't explore the riches they might find, as an early, huge snowstorm buried the mineral. The next spring, however, Hamlin's two younger brothers went to the spot and unearthed two bushels' worth of the green and red gem. (One of the boys was Hannibal Hamlin, who went on to become vice president of the United States in 1861.) The Mount Mica tourmaline mine became the site of the first commercial gem mine in the country, and it produced one crystal that weighed more than 30 pounds (14 kg). Later, the mine produced the world's first rose quartz. Mount Mica still produces tourmaline and other gems, and tourmaline is Maine's official state mineral.

OPAL
• CREATING COLORS •

I contain multitudes

et's make it crystal clear—some minerals aren't really minerals at all. Instead, they're what geologists call mineraloids, and opal is one of these. Sure, some opals are considered gemstones, and they might look like minerals. But on the inside, their atoms don't form crystal structures, like the atoms in minerals do. Instead, the silica in opals form tiny balls. And these balls help explain some of opal's appeal.

What we think of as white light is actually made up of different colors of light. As "white" light hits the tiny silica balls inside some opals, it splits into these different colors, so an opal can be quite a colorful gem. Only opals that have the silica balls neatly arranged and stacked will split the light and create colors.

PRECIOUS OR POTCH

The opals that produce a rainbow of colors are called precious opals. They have many different names, depending on the colors in them. Ones that are red, yellow, or orange are called fire opals. Most of these come from Mexico. Some opals are black, though they're rare. Many of these black ones come from Australia, which for years produced almost all the opal mined in the world. Now Ethiopia is becoming a major source of opals.

Only a small percentage of opals are precious and turned into gems. Most of them are what's called potch. These opals don't scatter light. In some opal jewelry, potch opals are placed behind the precious opal, to make the color even more dazzling.

A GEM OF A DISCOVERY

Some scientists think opals may hold clues to life on Mars. More than a century after a meteorite from Mars crashed northwest of Alexandria, Egypt, scientists used sophisticated new technology to learn that the space rock contained some fire opal. On Earth, as that kind of opal forms, it can trap tiny living creatures called microbes inside of it. (It's similar to how amber hardens around insects and other living things.) The scientists theorize that if fire opal can trap microbes on Earth, Martian microbes could be trapped in the fire opals on the red planet. Finding some of these microbes would prove that there was once life on Mars. Scientists at NASA first detected evidence of opals on Mars in 2008, thanks to data gathered and analyzed by the Mars Reconnaissance Orbiter.

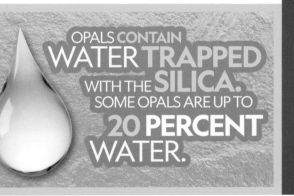

OPALS CONTAIN **WATER TRAPPED** WITH THE **SILICA.** SOME OPALS ARE UP TO **20 PERCENT WATER.**

WHERE IN THE WORLD? THE UNDERGROUND OPAL TOWN

Australia is called the "land down under" because it sits far south of the Equator. And down under parts of Australia there is a *lot* of opal. In 1915, miners looking for gold in South Australia found opal instead. Since then, some of the world's most famous opals have come from Coober Pedy, Australia's most famous mining town. One of them, the Olympic Australis, is the largest and most expensive opal in the world. Weighing a whopping 17,000 carats, it was valued at almost $2 million in 2017. Another Coober Pedy find was the Fire of Australia. This uncut opal is the size of a softball and weighs almost 5,000 carats. It has all the colors of the rainbow but is particularly rich in red. Coober Pedy is also known for how some of the residents live— underground! To escape the intense desert heat there, people have built underground homes, as well as churches and stores. That's *really* going down under!

OTHER POPULAR GEMS
• MORE GORGEOUS GEMS •

Here's a quick look at more popular gemstones that dazzle with their brilliant colors and beauty.

① AMETHYST

What mineral can produce something as plain as sand and as pretty as a gem? Quartz, of course. Pink quartz produces the gem called rose quartz, and purple quartz is the source of the gemstone amethyst. Its color comes from bits of iron in the mineral. St. Valentine—as in Valentine's Day—was said to have worn an amethyst ring with an image of Cupid carved into it. Since then, amethysts have been linked to love, just like the day named for the saint. One amethyst, however, got no love. The Delhi Purple Sapphire is actually an amethyst. One tall tale about the gem says it was stolen from a temple in India. After that, the people who owned it were said to have experienced bad luck, such as losing their jobs. Today, the gem is at London's Natural History Museum.

② CITRINE

Another gem of a quartz is citrine, the rarest gemstone from that mineral. Citrine gets its yellow color from small amounts of iron, and its name reflects that color—it comes from the Latin word for citrus, which refers to a tree that produces yellow fruit. Since citrine is so rare, some of the gems bearing that name are actually amethysts that have been heated to change their color to yellow or orange. It's sometimes considered the second birthstone for November, after topaz.

③ LAPIS LAZULI

Want a challenge? Try saying this gemstone's name three times fast, and you'll see why it's often called lapis for short. The best lapis comes from mines high in the mountains of Afghanistan, where some of the mines have been producing the stone for almost 3,000 years. Lapis has not just turned up in jewelry. For centuries, skilled carvers turned chunks of lapis into such items as bowls, combs, and even board games, like chess sets. When crushed, lapis makes a blue paint, and ancient Egyptians used crushed lazurite (lapis lazuli is the gem form of lazurite) for eye makeup.

④ GARNET

What gem is often red but can be a variety of colors? Gosh darn it, it's garnet! The name applies to several different minerals that turn up in all three varieties of rocks. People have been wearing garnet jewelry for more than 5,000 years. While most garnet gems are red, they can also be green or blue. One of the rarest types of garnet gemstones is tsavorite, a dark green form of grossular garnet found in East Africa.

⑤ TOPAZ

At one time, people confused topaz and citrine, since both are yellow. Topaz, though, is its own mineral, not a type of quartz, and it's one of the hardest minerals in the world. One natural shade of topaz is orangey red and is called imperial topaz, named for the past royal rulers of Russia. (Today imperial topaz is also the name for gems in different shades of pink and red.) The country once produced most of the world's imperial topaz, and the Russian rulers said only they and their families could wear it. Today, most imperial topaz comes from Brazil, including one of the largest cut yellow topaz stones. The gem weighs 10 pounds (4.5 kg) and is as big as a headlight on a car. It's one of the largest cut gemstones of any kind in the world.

BECOMING A ROCK HOUND
• DOGGEDLY HUNTING FOR ROCKS •

Stay curious!

Some hounds have a supersensitive sense of smell and can track people. Rock hounds do something similar—they track down samples of rocks and minerals for their collections. But unlike dogs, these hounds use their eyes and fingers to tell one find from another.

Because rocks and minerals are all around, a budding rock hound such as yourself could start looking for them close to home: in your backyard, on school grounds, or at a park. Just make sure that if you go onto private property, you get permission first. And be aware that even on many public lands, such as state and national parks, people are not allowed to disturb or remove rocks, minerals, or fossils. Around the world, people have even been arrested for taking rocks they shouldn't have!

• TOOLS OF THE TRADE •

Before they head out, rock hounds need the right equipment. Here's a basic list of what beginning rock collectors should have. Most of these items can be found at a well-equipped hardware store.

GEOLOGIST'S HAMMER:
Strike a blow for your collection with this essential tool. One end has a head like a regular hammer for breaking off pieces of a large rock. The other end has a pointy pick to dig into tight spaces. Some rock hounds also use a chisel with their hammer to break off rock samples.

A STIFF BRUSH:
This can help you brush away dirt from your sample.

POCKET MAGNIFIER:
Get up close and personal with your samples with this small magnifying glass. It will help you pick out the different kinds of minerals in a rock.

A BACKPACK:
You can't carry all this stuff *and* the rocks you find in your hands! A pack can also carry any food and water (always stay hydrated!) you may want to bring on your hunting expedition.

PROPER CLOTHING:
Protect yourself from flying pieces of rock with goggles, gloves, shoes with hard toes, and maybe a hard hat.

A GUIDEBOOK:
This reference book will tell you where you're likely to find particular rocks and minerals, as well as what they look like.

PEN AND PAPER:
You'll want to note where you found certain samples.

WHAT'S WHAT?

A guidebook can help you identify some rocks in the field, but certain tests can help you figure out what minerals you have. Special pieces of porcelain called streak plates can show the color a mineral leaves behind when rubbed against a plate. Vinegar can tell you if a rock has calcite in it, since the mineral fizzes when the acidic vinegar touches it. Special kits contain samples of rocks that range from soft to hard on the Mohs scale, and they can help you determine how hard a particular mineral is.

Once you identify what you've collected, you might want to show it off. Rock hounds sometimes store their samples in boxes with individual sections that can be mounted on walls. But even something as simple as an egg carton can hold what you find.

If you're new to collecting—more of a rock pup than a hound—you might want to consider joining a local rock and mineral club. Members share their knowledge and go out together to hunt for specimens. That last point is very important—**you shouldn't go out rock hunting alone!** Go with an adult or a group. That way you can share your interest in rocks and stay safe.

A listing of some of the rock clubs that welcome kids in each state is available at the American Federation of Mineralogical Societies website: **amfed.org/kids.htm**

179

GLOSSARY

SANDSTONE FORMATIONS
IN ANTELOPE CANYON,
ARIZONA, U.S.A.

ABRASIVE:
Substance used to smooth a rough surface.

AGGREGATE:
A crushed mixture of rocks.

ALLOY:
A compound made by combining two or more metals.

ARCHAEOLOGIST:
A scientist who studies the structures, tools, and other items left by ancient peoples.

CABOCHON:
Gemstones that are cut and polished but without facets; they sometimes feature a cat's eye formation.

CASTS:
Objects made by shaping molten metal (or similar material) in a mold.

CATALYSTS:
Substances that speed up how other chemicals react with each other.

COMPOUND:
A material formed when two or more chemical elements are combined.

CORRODE:
To wear away slowly because of a chemical reaction.

EXCAVATE:
To dig something out of the ground.

FACET:
A side or smooth face of a cut gemstone.

FOSSIL FUELS:
Oil, coal, and natural gas, which were formed from ancient plant and animal remains.

HYDROTHERMAL:
In geology, relating to the formation of minerals in hot water.

INCLUSIONS:
Tiny particles of material trapped in gems.

LUBRICANT:
A substance that makes solids easily slide against each other.

OBELISK:
A stone column that usually has four sides, often with a pyramid on its top.

ORE:
A rock or mineral mined for the metal it contains.

ORGANIC:
Relating to things that are or were once living, or to the carbon in living things.

PALEONTOLOGIST:
A scientist who studies past living creatures through fossils.

PRECIPITATE:
When a solid forms from either a liquid or gas.

RADIOACTIVE:
A substance that releases a form of energy called radiation.

SLAG:
The waste product created when smelting iron or other metals.

STRATA:
Layers of sediment or sedimentary rock.

SYNTHETIC:
Made in a laboratory or by machines.

TEPHRA:
A mixture of lava, hot ash, and pieces of rock.

VENT:
An opening in Earth's ocean crust.

Words I can get behind

INDEX

Boldface indicates illustrations.

PHOTO CREDITS

Many thanks to Ariane Szu-Tu and Jen Agresta for their expert editing and unending encouragement, and to Steve Tomecek for making sure everything was scientifically correct. And, as always, a salute to all my nieces and nephews who eagerly read my books!

— M. B.

Since 1888, the National Geographic Society has funded more than 14,000 research, conservation, education, and storytelling projects around the world. National Geographic Partners distributes a portion of the funds it receives from your purchase to National Geographic Society to support programs including the conservation of animals and their habitats. To learn more, visit natgeo.com/info.

For more information, visit nationalgeographic.com, call 1-877-873-6846, or write to the following address:

National Geographic Partners, LLC
1145 17th Street N.W.
Washington, D.C. 20036-4688 U.S.A.

For librarians and teachers: nationalgeographic .com/books/librarians-and-educators/

More for kids from National Geographic: natgeokids.com

National Geographic Kids magazine inspires children to explore their world with fun yet educational articles on animals, science, nature, and more. Using fresh storytelling and amazing photography, Nat Geo Kids shows kids ages 6 to 14 the fascinating truth about the world—and why they should care. kids.nationalgeographic.com/subscribe

For rights or permissions inquiries, please contact National Geographic Books Subsidiary Rights: bookrights@natgeo.com

Designed by Sanjida Rashid

The publisher would like to acknowledge the following people for making this book possible: Ariane Szu-Tu, editor; Jen Agresta, project editor; Michael Burgan, author; Sanjida Rashid, art director; Lori Epstein, photo director; Sarah J. Mock, senior photo editor; Danny Meldung/Photo Affairs, Inc., photo research; Joan Gossett, editorial production manager; Molly Reid, production editor; Anne LeongSon and Gus Tello, design production assistants; and Michelle Harris, fact-checker extraordinaire.

The publisher would also like to thank Steve Tomecek for his rock-solid expert review of this book.

Library of Congress Cataloging-in-Publication Data

Names: Burgan, Michael, author.
Title: Rocks and minerals / Michael Burgan.
Description: Washington, D.C. : National Geographic Kids, [2022] | Series: Weird but true know-it-all | Includes index. | Audience: Ages 8-12 | Audience: Grades 4-6
Identifiers: LCCN 2020000487 | ISBN 9781426371837 (paperback) | ISBN 9781426371844 (library binding)
Subjects: LCSH: Rocks--Juvenile literature. | Minerals--Juvenile literature.
Classification: LCC QE432.2 .B85 2022 | DDC 552--dc23
LC record available at https://lccn.loc .gov/2020000487

Printed in Hong Kong
21/PPHK/1